New Works in Accounting History

Series Editor

Richard P. Brief

Leonard N. Stern School of Business
New York University

A GARLAND SERIES

THE BEGINNINGS OF ACCOUNTING AND ACCOUNTING THOUGHT

Accounting Practice
in the Middle East
(8000 B.C . to 2000 B.C.)
and Accounting Thought
in India (300 B.C. and the
Middle Ages)

RICHARD MATTESSICH

GARLAND PUBLISHING, INC.
A MEMBER OF THE TAYLOR & FRANCIS GROUP
NEW YORK & LONDON / 2000

Published in 2000 by
Garland Publishing Inc.
A Member of the Taylor & Francis Group
19 Union Square West
New York, NY 10003

10   9   8   7   6   5   4   3   2   1

Library of Congress Cataloging-in-Publication Data
Mattessich, Richard.
    The beginnings of accounting and accounting throught : accounting prac-
tice in the Middle East (8000 B.C. to 2000 B.C.) and accounting thought in India (300 B.C. and the Middle Ages) / Richard Mattessich.
        p. cm. — (New works in accounting history)
    ISBN 0-8153-3445-1 (alk. paper)
    1. Accounting—Middle East—History. 2. Accounting—India—History.
I. Title. II. Series.
HF5616.M628.M378 2000
657'.0956—dc21   00-034726

Printed on acid-free, 250-year-life paper
Manufactured in the United States of America

In memory of my parents,
Gerda and Victor Mattessich

Contents

Foreword

Richard V. Mattessich has been a leading figure in accounting education and research for several decades. His varied interests include work on the development of an axiomatic approach to accounting postulates, computer simulation of the budgeting process, the accounting uses of matrix algebra and, more generally, the relationship between management science and accounting. His best-known work *Accounting and Analytical Methods*, was published in 1964 and it established Mattessich's reputation as one of the leading thinkers in the field of accounting. Writing in the January 1966 issue of *The Accounting Review*, W. W. Cooper, recommended this book "to all those who are concerned with exploring, repairing and extending ideas, practices, and principles that are fundamental to accounting." Cooper went on to say "that such persons will find that this book is seminal and important."

In recent years, Mattessich turned his attention to the beginnings of accounting and has published seven articles dealing with accounting practices in the Middle East from 8000 B.C. to 2000 B.C. and accounting thought in India from 300 B.C. and the Middle Ages. These papers raise many profound issues that have both philosophical and historical implications. Did Sumerian token-envelope accounting at the end of the forth millennium precede the written word and constitute a major impetus in the creation of writing and abstract counting? Was token-envelope accounting a prototype of a closed double-entry accounting system? The reader will find these and other questions raised by Mattessich thought provoking, to say the least.

As editor of the Garland series in accounting, I am pleased that these writings by Mattessich on accounting in antiquity are being brought together in one volume. This anthology will make the material more widely available and, therefore, it is much easier for students and researchers to study this important and fascinating subject.

Richard P. Brief
Leonard N. Stern School of Business
New York University
February 8, 1999

Preface

This book consists of a series of historical-archeological papers of mine, written between 1987 and 1998. They are organized in a sequence that offers a more or less chronological picture of the early stages of accounting and accounting thought.

The first section of the Introduction gives an over-view of the individual chapters, summarizing the major insights—which, of course, cannot reflect the details found in the individual chapters, so indispensable for a scientific understanding of the various historical events under consideration. Later sections of the Introduction deal with methodological and other philosophic issues. The book itself may be taken as a guide to further archeological and historical literature of our discipline, but it primarily constitutes an accountant's interpretation, as well as supplement, of striking and sometimes surprising archeological and historical findings. Thanks to the initiative of Professor Richard P. Brief and Garland Publishing, Inc., these papers are integrated to convey not only a sketch of the beginning of accounting practice but also of what, according to present knowledge, are the first descriptive and, in a way, "theoretical" thoughts on accounting.

This gives me the opportunity of acknowledging the stimulus I received from the path-breaking work of Prof. Denise Schmandt-Besserat, an archeologist of the University of Texas at Austin. I am also grateful for her advice, sought by myself in connection with several of my papers. Prof. Schmandt-Besserat is one of the founders of the archeology of accounting and the leading expert on token and token-envelopes, the precursors of cuneiform writing. I have been in correspondence with her for over a decade, and had the pleasure of meeting her personally a couple of times.

Special thanks go to Prof. Brief for his kind Foreword, as well as for reading the draft to the Preface and Introduction. Furthermore, I am grateful to the editors and publishers for permission to reprint here the following papers of mine: "Prehistoric Accounting and the Problem of Representation: On Recent Archeological Evidence of the Middle-East from 8000 B.C. to 3000 B.C.," *Accounting Historians Journal* 14 (2), Fall 1987, pp. 71-91; "Recent Insights into Mesopotamian Accounting of the 3rd Millennium B.C.—Successor to Token Accounting," *Accounting Historians Journal* 25 (1) June 1998, pp. 1-27, and "Follow-Up to 'Recent Insights into Mesopotamian Accounting of the 3rd Millennium B.C.' Correction to Table 1" *Accounting Historians Journal* 25 (2), pp. 147-149), "From Accounting to Negative Numbers: A Signal Contribution of Medieval India to Mathematics," *Accounting Historians Journal* 25 (2) December 1998, pp. 129-145; "Counting, Accounting, and the Input-Output Principle: Recent Archeological Evidence Revising Our View on the Evolution of Early Record Keeping" in O. Finley Graves, ed., *The Costing Heritage—Studies in Honor of S. Paul Garner* (Harrisonburg, VA: Academy of Accounting Historians, Monograph No. 6, 1991, pp. 25-49); "Archeology of Accounting and Schmandt-Besserat's Contribution," *Accounting, Business and Financial History* 4 (1), 1994, pp. 5-28, and "Review and Extension of Bhattacharyya's *Modern Accounting Concepts in Kautilya's Arthaśāstra*," *Accounting, Business and Financial History* 8 (2) 1998, pp. 191-209 (both, thanks to the additional permission by Routledge, London, copyright).

My thanks also extend to the following publishers and institutions granting permission for reproducing various exhibits: Musée de Louvre (Department des Antiqués Orientales), Paris, for illustrations of clay tokens (Exhibits 1 to 4 of Chapters 1 and 2); the University of Chicago Press, for reproducing passages quoted from H. J. Nissen, Peter Damerow and R. K. Englund (1993), *Archaic Book keeping—Early Writing Techniques of Economic Administration in the Ancient Near East*, as well as for reproducing Figures 1 to 4 (of Chapter 4); the University of Texas Press, for reproducing Figure 1 (of Chapter 3) as an adaptation from Denise Schmandt-Besserat (1992, vol.1, excerpts from pp. 143-148) *Before Writing—From Counting to Cuneiform*.

Finally, I should like to express my gratitude to the Social Sciences and Humanities Research Council for continuing support of my research, and to the Faculty of Commerce and Business Administration, particular to our Acting Dean, Prof. Derek Atkinson, for providing research facilities.

THE BEGINNINGS OF ACCOUNTING AND ACCOUNTING THOUGHT

Accounting Practice in the Middle East (8000 B.C. to 2000 B.C.)
and Accounting Thought in India (200 B.C. and the Middle Ages)

CHAPTER 1

Introduction

1. GENERAL EXPOSITION

To fully appreciate the meaning of a discipline and its cultural significance, some familiarity with its beginning and early development seems necessary. Yet, in the case of accounting and its first "theoretical" manifestations these beginnings were shrouded in obscurity for too long a time. Only during the last decade or two has this veil slowly been lifted.[1] Step by step, have accountants gained insight into the forces, techniques and circumstances that shaped the early phases of their discipline. Of course, it has been known for some time that these beginnings are to be found in antiquity or even prehistoric times, but what came as a total surprise was the knowledge that the origin of so humble a discipline as ours, had a most fundamental impact on the cultural life of humankind in general.

In the literature of accounting and accounting history it was, for example, taken for granted that writing and counting were prerequisites of record keeping (e.g., see Littleton 1966, p. 12; Skinner 1987, pp. 4-6). That this was a misconception is revealed through the revolutionary research of the French-American archeologist Schmandt-Besserat (e.g., 1977, 1992), bringing forth convincing evidence that Sumerian token-envelope accounting (for an explanation of this term, see below), at the end of the fourth millennium B.C., not only preceded the written word but constituted the major impetus in the creation of writing and abstract counting. There were also major changes of

Mesopotamian record keeping between 4000 B.C. and 2000 B.C., and these changes proved to be highly significant. All this refutes such previously held views as the one expressed by Keister:

> A functional approach, rather than a chronological approach, is necessary in the analysis of the records kept by Mesopotamians, because *there were almost no significant changes in the records between the years 4000 B.C. and 538 B.C.* the date that the second Babylonian empire fell to the Persians . . . the passage of years saw more particulars entered on the records, the totals were less frequently incorrect, information known to everyone was not written down as often, and the dating system became more precise and accurate, *but, other than these relatively unimportant changes, the records remained quite unchanged.* (Keister 1963, p. 372; my italics).[2]

Contrary to this quote, the new insights show that during this period a series of innovations, each fundamental in its own right, did take place. Around 3250 B.C. Sumerian scribes preserved the clay tokens (representing commodities and originally stored in perishable containers) in burned clay envelopes (hollow clay balls or bullae), thus converting token accounting into what I refer to as "token-envelope accounting". In addition, perforated tokens on sealed strings were used as an alternative aggregation device for special purposes. Soon afterwards, around 3200 B.C., the accounting tokens were impressed upon the outer surface before putting them into the envelopes and sealing the latter.[3] This not only enabled the recognition of the token content without breaking the envelope, it also introduced a double recording in so far as the same quantity was recorded twice: first, *inside* the envelope through individually movable tokens (as assets), and second, on the *outside* as a totality of inseparable token-impressions (as equity).

During the third millennium B.C. further striking accounting innovations can be found. Apart from introducing labor and cost accounting, agricultural and real estate accounting, budgeting, etc., the clay envelopes were abandoned and replaced by flat clay tablets to be impressed by tokens which then merely transferred symbols, but had no longer representative meaning on their own. Later, the quantitative token-impressions were supplemented by incised symbols carrying qualitative information. Only then could the process of developing various stages of proto-cuneiform and cuneiform writing begin.

2. REMARKS ON INDIVIDUAL CHAPTERS

Each paper is assigned to a separate chapter (with the exception of two articles in Chapter 5 which belong together). Chapters 2 to 5 deal with accounting practice in the Middle East over a time span of some 6000 years (from about the ninth millennium B.C. to the end of the third millennium B.C.), while Chapters 6 and 7 deal with the more "theoretical" development of accounting in India around the turn from the fourth to the third millennium B.C. and some aspect of Medieval India.

Chapter 2: "Prehistoric Accounting and the Problem of Representation: On Recent Archeological Evidence of the Middle-East from 8000 B.C. to 3000 B.C." Accounting can be traced back some 10,000 years in the Middle East, and writing as well as abstract counting apparently emerged from the Sumerian token-envelope accounting of the 4th and early 3rd millenium B.C. The last stage of this early accounting technique represented individual assets through clay tokens inside a clay envelope and showed their sum-total (as a kind of equity) in form of a set of inseparable token impressions on the surface of the clay envelope. Thus, this paper discusses token accounting (including what I now call "token-envelope accounting"), and interprets it from an accountant's point of view, illuminating it within the modern cultural setting. Special emphasis is put on two points:

(i) That token accounting not only preceded cuneiform writing but constituted the underlying matrix out of which writing in general arose. This may well be the first major civilizing contribution of accounting to humankind.

(ii) The relation between reality and its conceptual representation in thoughts, symbols and words has been one of the major topics of philosophy. A prehistoric system in which clay tokens stand for "real" objects (like cloth, labor, sheep, silver, wool, etc.) may well be suited to explain the transition from pictographic (concrete) to ideographic (abstract) representation, and even from "showing" to "saying," to use Wittgenstein's terminology. Indeed, many symbols of token accounting were still pictographic while others were already ideographic. Hence in the second half of this paper, I tried to relate the phenomenon of token accounting to modern philosophy, particularly to Wittgenstein's two philosophies and the distinction between "showing" and "saying"—not least the transition from one to the other, as revealed in token accounting.

Chapter 3: "Counting, Accounting, and the Input-Output Principle: Recent Archeological Evidence Revising our View on the Evolution of Early Record Keeping" overlaps somewhat with the preceding paper (particularly as far as Exhibits 1 to 4 are concerned), but here the thrust is less on philosophic-representational problems and less on token accounting as the foundation of cuneiform writing, but more on Schmandt-Besserat's claim that token accounting preceded abstract counting. The paper also contains further interpretation of the "token system" from an accountant's point of view. It emphasizes the distinction between physical and social reality and shows that the double classification of accounting arises not from one duality, but from three (or at least two) distinct but interconnected kinds (first, physical transfers of commodities; second, debt claims, connecting a debtor to a creditor; and third, ownership rights, connecting a person to an economic good).

Chapter 4: "Archeology of Accounting and Schmandt-Besserat's Contribution" is, first of all, a discussion of Schmandt-Besserat's (1992) two volumes' *magnum opus*, in which most of her "token research" is meticulously described and illustrated (since this time, she published two further books on this subject: Schmandt-Besserat 1996, 1997). The paper offers, among other material, a list of almost 40 concepts, juxtaposing their symbols in token-form as well as in form of impressions on the later cuneiform tablets. This illustrates Schmandt-Besserat's ingenious feat of "retroactively" inferring the meaning of many three-dimensional tokens from the very similarly looking but two-dimensional imprints (the connotation of which was, by this time, already known). My own interpretations are here further extended and supported by various exhibits (see Figure 1 and Appendices A, B). For readers interested in observing the development of my personal thoughts on token and token-envelope accounting, a comparison between the individual Chapters 2 to 5 may prove of some interest. In each of the corresponding papers, I have tried to probe these issues from a somewhat different angle.

Chapter 5: "Recent Insights into Mesopotamian Accounting of the 3rd Millennium B.C. — Successor to Token Accounting" and "Follow-Up to 'Recent Insights into Mesopotamian Accounting of the 3rd Millennium B.C.' — Correction to Table 1" extend the discussion of archeological accounting research (from the period of 8000 B.C. to 3000 B.C.) into the third millennium B.C. (up to 2000 B.C.), which indicates further portentous accounting developments. As the tokens were now impressed onto clay tablets (and not on cumbersome clay envelopes with tokens inside), the tokens lost their conceptual function and became mere tools. Later, the quantitative token-impressions were supplemented by incised symbols carrying qualitative information. Then a lengthy process began during which the token-impressions as well as the incised marks were converted into the different stages of proto-cuneiform and cuneiform writing (originally limited to recording commercial and economic transactions, but later used for literary purposes as well).

It is remarkable that, similar to token-envelope accounting, proto-cuneiform accounting records show on one side the charges or debit entries and on the reverse side the discharges or credit entries (cf. Nissen et al. 1993). However, there is no evidence that would connect the latter procedure to a closed double-entry system (in contrast to token-envelope accounting were such evidence does exist). Obviously, a clay envelope was a simple enough device to practically guarantee that all tokens inside were impressed on the outside of the envelope. But the innumerable clay tablets of a single bookkeeping system could no longer sustain such a genuine and closed double-entry feature without any particular effort. The feature of revealing on the outside the content was no more needed when using tablets, and other advantages of the double-entry feature were, apparently, not exploited by the Sumerians. Yet, it is precisely this feature of archaic bookkeeping which reinforces my hypothesis about the double-entry feature of the preceding token-envelope accounting.

Apart from those innovations, better techniques permitted increasing refinements in accounting, be it through the use of numerous number systems (each for a different task), be it for surprisingly sophisticated costing and budgeting procedures, applied to a variety of different areas (from construction activities to agriculture and cattle husbandry). Thanks to the primarily interpretive archeological research, revealed in Nissen, Damerow and Englund (1993), new vistas have been opened that call for further interpretation from an accountant's point of view. My paper has begun with this task, and hopefully others will follow suit.

Chapter 6: "Review and Extension of Bhattacharyya's *Modern Accounting Concepts in Kautilya's Arthaśāstra*" makes three great leaps. First, a chronological one, from the third millennium B.C. to the fourth century B.C.; second, a geographical one, from Mesopotamia to the heartland of India; and third, an intra-disciplinary one, from accounting practice to accounting thought. The paper is not merely a review article of Bhattacharyya's (1988) book, with additional reference to Choudhury (1982), it also brings notions of modern inflation accounting into play and gives further interpretations. It thus offers, as far as present evidence affords, a glance into the very first descriptive or perhaps "theoretical" reflections on accounting, as presented in the *Arthasāstra* by Kautilya Vishnugupta, around 300 B.C. This Hindu sage not only distinguished between different types of income, he mentions concepts that invoke resemblance to the real vs. fictitious gains, fixed vs. variable costs, classifies expenses and is heavily concerned with taxation issues—and all this, some two thousand years or more before Western accountants developed similar ideas.

Chapter 7: "From Accounting to Negative Numbers: A Signal Contribution of Medieval India to Mathematics" looks at some relations between mathematics and accounting. However, in contrast to previous studies, it does not look at the aid which accounting may have derived from mathematics. It rather examines the reverse, namely, whether mathematics may have benefitted from previously existing accounting notions. In particular, the paper tries to show that the Hindus' early concern with accounting thought seems to have contributed to the acceptance of negative numbers by Indian mathematicians of the Middle Ages (about a thousand years earlier than the acceptance of those numbers in Western mathematics). What ought to be of particular interest to accountants is that medieval Indian mathematicians justified this practice by regarding a debt as a negative, and an asset as a positive quantity. The paper hypothesizes a connection between the use of such accounting (and legal) notions as debts and assets by Indian mathematicians, on one side, and the previous accounting achievements on the Indian subcontinent, on the other side (see preceding chapter). The paper also examines the evidence supporting this hypothesis. For example, the translation of a medieval Indian manuscript, the *Áchárya* by Bhāskara (1151—see Colebrooke 1817/1973) contains evidence that Indian mathematicians assigned negative numbers to debts and positive ones to assets. Even more important, this practice—possibly influenced by the relatively sophisticated tradition of Indian accounting, as described above—was used to justify the acceptance of negative numbers (in contrast to Europe, which then lagged so much behind).

3. METHODOLOGY

There seem to exist some methodological misunderstandings among accountants and accounting historians as to the "speculative" nature of historical and even scientific hypotheses. Before presenting my papers let me shed light on this issue by invoking in this and the next section some aspects of the philosophy of science in general, and of history in particular. Science, by its very nature, is speculative; and absolute truth is an ideal to be aimed for—at best to be approximated, but hardly ever to be attained. And if attained, no one would be sure about such attainment. Every scientific and historical theory or view is hypothetical. Indeed, Hume's scepticism, destructive of pure empiricism has—despite many unsuccessful attempts (from Kant to Carnap and beyond)—still to find a satisfactory refutation.[4]

This dilemma results in a neuralgic point concerning the evidential support which a particular theory or hypothesis can command. Intuitively, we feel that it is the difference in their "strength" which should enable us to rank theories and hypotheses within science and history and, perhaps even more important, draw the boundaries between the following three areas: scientific speculation, philosophic speculation, and wild, unsupported speculation.

But first, our mind is constructed in such a way that all of its representative activity depends on reduction and simplifications that can be deceptive—and not only in everyday life, but also in art, religion, philosophy, history and even in the hard sciences. We cannot but accept this uncomfortable fact. All the more reason to be on guard of the illusions created by the simplifying assumptions of our theories, no less than of other selective features inherent in our perceptive and conceptive apparatus.

Second, despite the enormous effort by Carnap (e.g., 1962) and others to create a probabilistic *theory of confirmation*, there are still no generally accepted and reliable rules for establishing the strength with which some facts support an hypothesis. On the other hand, the well-known practice of statistical hypothesis testing by means of a *degree of confidence*, though widely used, could not either get rid of the major logical problem. This practice too has no firm foundation in the philosophy of knowledge, it cannot confirm any causal relationship but merely reinforces, on purely *psychological* grounds (as Hume anticipated more than a quarter of a millennium ago), the confidence in a possibly causal link. But the fact that this is a statistical and even an "objective" method (at least wherever mass phenomena are involved) deceives many a scholar about its epistemic status. Nevertheless, it may be the best pragmatic tool available for coming to grips with this knotty problem, at least in a limited number of situations. But wherever repeatable statistical mass phenomena are not available, as in most of historical research, statistical hypothesis testing is of little use.

Third, in addition to these difficulties, the historical sciences (archeology, paleontology, political and cultural history, etc.) as well as the applied sciences (accounting, engineering, law, medicine, etc.) are often confronted with choosing from two or more hypotheses, *none of which may have particularly strong support*. In such a case, one is forced to evaluate the strength of support on even more shaky grounds, and then choose the best alternative, as weakly supported as it might be. Then it becomes obvious that the traditional practice of ranking hypotheses has to be supplemented with Popper's falsificational approach. That is to say, one must try to refute or "falsify" the hypothesis believed to be best supported. But as long as oneself or anyone else cannot find a valid refutation, one may preliminarily accept it.

Fourth, an important factor in the preliminary acceptance or rejection of an hypothesis, particularly an historical one, is the extent to which it coheres with related facts and theories. In addition to other requirements, it is necessary to take those facts and theories into account. Thus, I find myself in agreement with Bunge's (1983a, pp. 94-198; 1983b, pp. 58-154) "critical realism" which calls for *multiple testing* procedures that encompass not only the "coherence theory" of rationalism, but also the "positive evidence" of empiricism, and the "lack of negative evidence" of critical rationalism. I have relied upon such combined methodology, wherever I defended an historical hypothesis, be it one advanced by others, such as Bhattacharyya, Nissen and his team, Schmandt-Besserat, or by myself.

4. FURTHER PHILOSOPHIC CONSIDERATIONS OF HISTORY

There exist several approaches of writing history; one of the most prevalent has been to concentrate on the accumulation of raw facts (or what one takes to be for facts). Obviously, many scholars disagree with this approach; they argue that history cannot do without interpretation. But interpretation is always rooted in some philosophical precept; and anyone attempting to do historical research—whether he is a professionally trained historian or not—is obliged to reveal the kind of orientation or bias that may have influenced his findings.

I believe the obsession with pure facts not only results in boring history but also deceives the reader about an assumed degree of objectivity that no history can truthfully claim. And, in the words of the well-known British historian, E. H. Carr (1964, p. 20), "those historians who today pretend to dispense with a philosophy of history are merely trying, vainly and self-consciously, like members of a nudist colony, to create the Garden of Eden in their garden suburbs." This author also reiterates and paraphrases the following thoughts of Collingwood (1945), one of the most renowned philosopher of history:

> But a past act is dead, i.e., meaningless to the historian, unless he can understand the thought that lay behind it. Hence 'all history is the history of thought', and 'history is the re-enactment in the historian's mind of the thought whose history he is studying'. The reconstitution of the past in the historian's mind is dependent on empirical evidence. But it is not in itself an empirical process, and cannot consist in a mere recital of facts. On the contrary, the process of reconstitution governs the selection and interpretation of the facts: this, indeed, is what makes them historical facts. (Carr 1964, p. 22)

And whoever craves for a more original way of conveying similar sentiments, may turn to the renowned Italian play-write, Luigi Pirandello, who put the following words into the mouth of one of his characters (the "father"—towards the end of the first act) of his "Six Characters in Search of An Author": "But a fact is like a sack which won't stand up when it is empty. In order that it may stand up, one has to put [something] into it...." (Pirandello 1951, p. 391).

Even if I do not share all the maxims of such "idealistic" historians as Carr and Collingwood, I cannot deny the indispensability and importance of subjectively-tainted historical interpretation. And this despite the fact, or perhaps because of it, that I regard historical research as no less a search for truth than science. Between history and science, there may be important methodological differences (as to generalizability, etc.), but the ultimate goal is surely the same: to approximate what one hopes to be truth, in as rigorous and honest a way, as one is capable of. But no human being can do this without at least some personal judgments. This is precisely why no history or other science can be an individual undertaking; it must be a social enterprise, inculcated with a dialectical process of not merely personal but, above all, a collective soul-searching, constantly adjusting and readjusting for all kinds of biases, be they those of individuals, of fashions, or technical-scientific limitations, etc. Only through such dialectics is it possible to keep one's bearing on that lofty objective which all authentic truth-seekers pursue. In holding such a view, I might be regarded by some colleagues as belonging to the synthesis-oriented *"Annales* school" of history (see, Foster 1978, and Luft 1997, pp. 167-168—in contrast to the predominantly descriptive "narrative school," on one side, and the strongly analytical *"cliometrics* school," on the other side), but I am reluctant to be pigenholed, and prefer to count myself to none of these schools.

5. OTHER CONSIDERATIONS AND MISUNDERSTANDINGS

On more specific grounds there arises the question whether interpretation, once accepted as a legitimate activity of historians, is more important than fact-finding. This seems to me a very personal matter, some historians are better in collecting factual details while others may have a better intuition, seeing relationships which mere facts do not reveal. But searching for facts and interpretations are complementary and intertwining activities; neither can exist without the other. Accounting historians, particularly "factualists," not only manifest a degree of disregard towards accounting interpretations, but sometimes fail to see that a good deal of archeological research is no less interpretive. By no means do I deny that archeologists, like Schmandt-Besserat, Nissen, Damerow, Englund, etc., did a good deal of factual research. But by carefully reading their publications one gets the impression that at least as much of their research has distinctly interpretive features.

A very different controversy is hidden behind the question of what constitutes double-entry accounting. Some scholars seem to take exception to my view of regarding the Sumerian token-envelope accounting as a prototype of closed "double-entry accounting." To resolve this issue one first has to clarify what this expression really means. Indeed, there exist many definitions of it, and all too easily one can get mired in fruitless semantical controversies. But there is one escape from senseless debates: to recognize that there exists a hierarchy of double-entry systems from token-envelopes to modern accounting. All those systems possess a closed loop of entries with their respective counter-entries, yet each having its own characteristics, usually adding new features beyond the preceding stage.

Some accountants may even consider the presence of one or a few entries with corresponding counter-entries as a sufficient criterion. Indeed, this might qualify as a preparatory stage or even as the lowest stage—as controversial as it might seem to be. It may even be rooted in the thought that "DEB [double entry bookkeeping] was inherent in the two-sided nature of business transactions" (Yamey 1996, p. 218; cf., de Roover 1955, p. 405). But for me, a recording system in which every entry has its counter-entry (individually or globally), certainly qualifies as a prototype of genuine double-entry. And token-envelope accounting not only possesses such an input-output feature, it also expresses another duality by juxtaposing individual asset-tokens (inside the envelope) to a global equity in form of token-impressions (on the surface of the envelope). This asset/equity duality seems to me the most fundamental aspect. Such a view need not contradict the statement by Littleton and Zimmerman (1962, p. 47) that "[t]he significance of the accomplishment of integration of real and nominal accounts far surpasses every other single aspect of accounting development." But even if this is the case, one must not forget that such "integration" rests on the asset/equity duality, and is merely a further extension and division of owners' equity. The underlying dichotomy that every asset is bound to an equity claim (be it debt or owner's equity) is undoubtedly more basic. Whether it is also more "significant" may be a matter of opinion. But income can be determined through the equity account alone; and those who recognize only a system as "double-entry" which exhibits a separate income account (concentrating on the modern duality of "balance sheet vs. income statement"), overlook that such dualities as "input-output" and "asset/equity" are more fundamental.[5] The former found its first manifestation in the transfer of accounting tokens, and the latter found its inscriptive expression in token-envelope accounting; even if it arose incidentally out of the convenience of discerning quickly the content from the surface of the clay envelope. The Sumerians, or whoever created token accounting, were well aware of such legal relationships as debt and ownership, as well as the fact that the recording of an asset requires, in addition, a statement of the equity relation to some person or institution. In the face of such evidence, statements of the following kind may no longer be tenable: "even the most advanced of those civilizations [of the ancient world] failed to produce a double entry system or anything like it" (Chatfield 1974, p. 15). But twenty-five years ago accountants were not aware of token-envelope accounting, and it is in the nature of science to revise previous insights; there is no need to worry about past misconceptions as long as new evidence is admitted.

6. CONCLUSION

I hope the historical reflections in this book may help to disseminate relatively new insights about our discipline. But my aspirations extend further, for I believe this to be a particularly appropriate time to talk about millennia long past. Standing on the threshold of a new century, even a new millennium, we find ourselves in the grip of an ahistorical, perhaps even anti-historical, mentality, too much self-absorbed in the present and its immediate consequences. Most of us are too busy to contemplate the mystery of humankind. Indeed, a better understanding of it requires a more mature and long-run point of view; an outlook, not limited by a single life time, not even restricted to the last couple of centuries, but one that spans millennia and, ultimately, millions of years. Should we not try to comprehend all this by looking at every facet of our history, not merely military and political history in a linear or two-dimensional way? In taking a more long-term and multidimensional view, we may gain more than a chunk of historical knowledge; we may understand ourselves, not merely as the fragment of one's momentary existence, but as a whole, as the life of a species, the future of which has never been more uncertain than on the threshold of the third millennium A.D. Looking into the mirror of time may help us to comprehend the forces which, sooner or later, in one way or the other, are bound to prevent the sheer endless exponential growth of a single species. Such reflections may promote the wisdom necessary to preserving the earth that sustains us, instead of yielding to the dreams of our relentless ambitions.

NOTES

1. Older publications on early accounting history—such as that by Melis (1950), probably the most prominent among them—did not and could not reveal crucial details here presented, partly because archeological and other historical research was not yet in a position to supply the relevant "raw material."

2. Keister (1963) refers to Melis (1950) in support of his own view; but Melis comprehensive accounting history (covering several millennia) sounds much more cautious, as the pertinent quote shows:

> Thus, it seems to me, that the period between the pre-Sargon texts and those of Larsa indicate the road of the major development and of the highest mental accounting achievements inherited by posterity... (Melis 1950, p. 235; translated).

3. "Token accounting" is an expression used or coined by Schmandt-Besserat. It refers to a recording system employed in the area of the Fertile Crescent from ca. 8000 B.C. until ca. 3000 B.C. which used small clay tokens of different shapes. Thereby, each shape represented a different commodity (in the case of bulk goods, like grain, it was connected to a specific quantity). At a subsequent stage of this accounting system, sealed hollow clay balls ("envelopes") were employed to preserve those tokens, which before inserting, were impressed on the surface of the envelope. This latter system I shall address as "token-envelope accounting," as I believe that the distinction

between these two stages is important enough to assign different but related names.

4. As Bertrand Russell stated: "The principle itself [of induction].... must therefore be, or be deduced from, an independent principle not based upon experience. To this extent, Hume has proved that pure empiricism is not a sufficient basis for science. But if this principle is admitted, everything else can proceed in accordance with the theory that all knowledge is based on experience. It must be granted that this is a serious departure from pure empiricism, and that those who are not empiricists may ask why, if one departure is allowed, others are to be forbidden." Russell (1960), p. 674.

5. In non-monetary economies the distinction between a debt-equity and an ownership equity is often blurred. Assume, for example, some temple administrators hand over a herd of sheep to a farmer, who is obliged to return this herd (possibly by paying some "fee" in kind) after a year. Is this claim—recorded by putting the tokens of the sheep into a clay envelope, closed with the farmer's seal and stored in the temple—a debt or an ownership relation? If it conveys that the farmer is obliged to return exactly the same sheep, it seems to be an ownership claim (of the temple vis-a-vis the farmer), but if only an equivalent amount of sheep has to be returned, it could be taken for a debt claim.

REFERENCES(see also "References" at the end of each paper)

Bhattacharyya, Anjan K. (1988) *Modern Accounting Concepts in Kautilya's Artha÷#stra*, Calcutta: Firma KLM Private Ltd.

Bunge, Mario (1983a) *Treatise on Basic Philosophy, vol. 5— Epistemology & Methodology I*, Dordrecht-Holland: D. Reidel Publishing Company.

Bunge, Mario (1983b) *Treatise on Basic Philosophy, vol. 6— Epistemology & Methodology II*, Dordrecht-Holland: D. Reidel Publishing Company.

Carnap, Rudolph (1962), *Logical Foundations of Probability, 2nd ed.*, Chicago, IL: University of Chicago Press (first edition, 1950).

Carr, E. H. (1964), *What is History?* Harmondsworth, UK: Penguin Books, Ltd.

Chatfield, Michael (1974), *A History of Accounting Thought*, Hindsdale, IL: Dryden Press.

Chatfield, Michael and Richard Vangermeersch, eds. (1996), *The History of Accounting—An International Encyclopedia*, New York: Garland Publishing, Inc.

Choudhury, N. (1982) "Aspects of Accounting and Internal Control—India 4th century B.C.," *Accounting and Business Research* 46 (Spring): 105-110.

Collingwood, Rob (1945), *The Idea of History*, collected papers with a Foreword by T. M. Knox, Oxford.

De Roover, Raymond (1955), "New Perspectives of the History of Accounting," *The Accounting Review* 20 (July 1955), pp. 405-520.

Foster, R., "The *Annales* School," *Journal of Economic History* 38 (March 1972), pp. 309-337.

Kautilya (Vishnugupta) (around 300 B.C.), *Arthaśāstra* (India); for translations see for example: Kangle, R. P. (1963) *The Kautilya Arthaśāstra, Part II, An English Translation with Critical and Explanatory Notes*, Bombay: University of Bombay; later edition 1972.

Keister, Orville R. (1963), "Commercial Record-Keeping in Ancient Mesopotamia", *The Accounting Review* 6 (April), pp. 371-376.

Littleton, A. C. (1966), *Accounting Evolution to 1900*, New York: Russell and Russell; first edition, New York: American Institute of Publishing Company, 1933.

Littleton, A. C. and Vernon Zimmerman (1962), *Accounting Theory: Continuity and Change*, Englewood Cliffs, NJ: Prentice-Hall, Inc.

Luft, Joan, "Long-Term Change in Management Accounting: Perspectives from Historical Research," *Journal of Management Accounting Research* 9 (1997), pp. 163-197.

Mattessich, Richard (see "Preface")

Melis, Federigo (1950), *Storia della Ragioneria*, Bologna: Dott. Cesare Zuffi, editore.

Nissen, H. J., Damerow, Peter, and Englund, R. K. (1993), *Archaic Bookkeeping — Early Writing Techniques of Economic Administration in the Ancient Near East*, Chicago, IL: University of Chicago Press; Paul Larsen (trans.).

Pirandello, Luigi (1951), "Six Characters in Search of an Author" (translated by Edward Storer) in John Gassner, ed., *A Treasure of the Theatre, vol. 2, Revised Edition*, New York: Simon and Schuster, pp. 387-408.

Russell, Bertrand (1960), *A History of Western Philosophy*, New York: Simon & Schuster.

Skinner, Ross M. (1987), *Accounting Standards in Evolution*, Toronto, ON: Holt, Rinehart and Winston.

Schmandt-Besserat, Denise (1977), "An Archaic Recording System and the Origin of Writing," *Syro-Mesopotamian Studies*, Vol. 1, No. 2: 1-32.

Schmandt-Besserat, Denise (1979), "Reckoning Before Writing," *Archeology*, Vol. 32, No. 3: 23-31.

Schmandt-Besserat, Denise (1983), "Tokens and Counting," *Biblical Archeologist*, Vol. 46: 117-120.

Schmandt-Besserat, Denise (1992), *Before Writing*, Vol. I, *From Counting to Cuneiform*; Vol. II, *A Catalogue of Near Eastern Tokens*, Austin, TX: University of Texas Press.

Schmandt-Besserat, Denise (1996), *How Writing Came About*, 1st abridged edition of vol. I (1992) , Austin, TX: University of Texas Press.

Schmandt-Besserat, Denise (1997), *The History of Counting*, New York: Morrow, Junior Books.

Yamey, Basil S. (1947), "Notes on the Origin of Double Entry Bookkeeping," *The Accounting Review* 22 (July), pp. 263-272.

Yamey, Basil S. (1996), "Double Entry Bookkeeping, Origins," in M. Chatfield and R. Vangermeersch, eds., *The History of Accounting—An International Encyclopedia*. New York: Garland Publishing, Inc., pp. 218-219.

CHAPTER 2

Prehistoric Accounting and the Problem of Representation
On Recent Archeological Evidence of the Middle-East from 8000 B.C. to 3000 B.C.

The Accounting Historians Journal
Vol. 14, No. 2
Fall 1987

Richard Mattessich
UNIVERSITY OF BRITISH COLUMBIA

PREHISTORIC ACCOUNTING AND THE PROBLEM OF REPRESENTATION: ON RECENT ARCHEOLOGICAL EVIDENCE OF THE MIDDLE-EAST FROM 8000 B.C. TO 3000 B.C.

Abstract: Recent archeological research offers revolutionary insight about the precursor of abstract counting and pictographic as well as ideographic writing. This precursor was a data processing system in which *simple* (and later complex) *clay tokens* of various shapes were aggregated in *hollow clay receptacles or envelopes* (and later *sealed string systems*) to represent symbolically assets and economic transactions. Scores of such tokens (the recent explanation of which is due to Prof. Schmandt-Besserat) were found by archeologists all over the Fertile Crescent in layers belonging to the time between 8000 B.C. to 3100 B.C. — after this date cuneiform clay tablets emerged.

The economic-philosophic implications of this discovery are important. First, it suggests that *accounting preceded abstract counting as well as writing.* Second, it suggests that *conceptual representation* emerged gradually. Third, it confirms the previous hypotheses that *counting* emerged in *several stages.* Fourth, it reveals the existence of an *abstract input-output principle* some 10,000 years ago and a kind of double entry over 5,000 years ago. Finally, it offers the earliest illustration of the (occasional) validity of the *correspondence theory.*

To assist readers I have inserted at the beginning of the fifth section some explanatory paragraphs on Wittgenstein's work.

Introduction

The quest for the *origin of symbolic representation* is not unrelated to Wittgenstein's perennial question: How is lan-

This paper was initially presented as "Wittgenstein and Archeological Evidence of Representation and Data Processing from 8000 B.C. to 3000 B.C." at the 12th International Wittgenstein Symposium (Kirchberg/Wechsel, Austria) in August 1987. It is reproduced with permission of the General Editor of the Wittgenstein Publication Series, Elisabeth Leinfellner, and the publishing house, Hölder-Pichler-Tempskey, Vienna. Financial support by the Social Sciences and Humanities Research Council of Canada for this project, and the valuable correspondence with Professor Schmandt-Besserat are acknowledged.

21

guage possible? Indeed a disclosure of the historical roots of representation might lead to a novel and empirical answer to Wittgenstein's major query — at least as far as *written* language is concerned.

During the last decade Professor Schmandt-Besserat, an archeologist at the University of Texas in Austin [1978, 1980, 1981, 1981a, 1982, 1984, 1986, 1986a] has shed much light on the origin of writing and counting.[1] I shall concisely recapitulate the history and results of her research[2] and offer interpretations of it from a philosophic as well as economic point of view.

Symbolic Representation and the Evolution of Writing

The invention of writing has long been shrouded in awe and mystery. Over the centuries many unsuccessful attempts have been made to explain the origin of this event [Schmandt-Besserat 1986, pp. 31-32] until in the early 19th century archeological expeditions to Mesopotamia began to clarify this problem by hard and fast evidence. A pictographic limestone tablet unearthed at Kish, dating from about 3000 B.C.[3] is usually regarded as the earliest piece of writing known. But such isolated pictographs are very rare. In contrast to them are the oldest collections of clay tablets found in great quantities in Uruk (the biblical Erek), dating from 3100 B.C. The writing they contain is predominantly *ideographic* (abstract) intermingled with only occasional pictographic signs (sketches of objects such as a plow, chariot, sledge, boar, etc.) — but at this stage the boundary between ideographic and pictographic signs is blurred, and interpretations vary. This ideographic nature of early cuneiform writing from the 4th millennium B.C. was already recognized by Falkenstein [1936, p. 25], the first person to investigate them.[4] The meaning of this early or

---

[1]For details about the individual contributions of A. Leo Oppenheim, Pierre Amiet, Denise Schmandt Besserat, and others to the clarification of the origin of writing and the record keeping use of clay envelopes and string aggregates, see: Schmandt-Besserat [1980, pp. 358-361] as well as Jasim and Oates [1986, p. 348]. For a somewhat different interpretation see Vallat [1986, pp. 334-337].

[2]The *recapitulation* is mainly based on Schmandt-Besserat [1986].

[3]Mallowan [1961, p. 67] as well as Hawkes [1963, p. 378] still state this date with 3500 B.C.

[4]Falkenstein [1964, p. 11] also emphasizes that the invention of cuneiform writing is the invention of the Sumerians, and that it was created exclusively for the recording of *economic transactions*.

archaic writing is still an enigma, partly because of its ideo-graphic nature, partly because most ideographs could not be traced back to the later cuneiform writing of the first and second millennium B.C. — only the ideographs for sheep, oil, metal, labourer, measures of grain, animal and a few others were traceable.

The *abstract form* of these symbols as well as the *large repertory* of them (over a thousand different signs) combined with the scarcity of preceding pictographs posed a vexing question as to the evolution of writing. Surely it cannot have happened overnight, it must have gradually evolved. Yet where was the missing link, where was the prototype? It seems plausible that writing started with a relatively small number of pictographs, which gradually increased in number, slowly changing into ideographs. Out of lack of any evidence, it was hypothesized that the proto-writing must have been on perishable material and thus lost to posterity [Diringer 1968, p. 19].

However, Schmandt-Besserat advanced a much better substantiated and more plausible hypothesis. She noticed (from 1969 onwards) on occasion of visits to many archeological sites and museums an unexpectedly large number of odd and hitherto unexplained artifacts of various shapes to which she refers as "tokens" and among which she distinguished two major types: the earlier *plain tokens* (spheres, disks, cylinders, triangles, rectangles, cones, ovoids, and tetrahedrons) from ca. 8000 B.C. onwards, and the later *complex tokens* (variously incised or punctated and usually perforated, also of a greater variety of forms — *added* shapes: e.g. vessel forms, parabolas and bent coils). These small, ubiquitous objects (ca. 1 to 4 cm. across) were carefully hand-molded of clay and hardened by

Exhibit 1

1. Plain clay tokens

burning at a relatively low temperature (of ca. 600° C). At some sites only small numbers of these tokens were preserved, but at other sites (e.g. at Jarmo, Iraq, dated 6500 B.C.) some 1500 specimens were unearthed. Whether in Israel, Syria, Iraq, Turkey or Iran those artifacts were present all over the Middle East in layers dating from ca. 8000 to 3000 B.C. and even later. This ubiquity and wide dispersion obviously pointed at their religious, cultural or economic importance; but what was this important function? All archeologists and experts working in this area encountered these tokens, but none had a satisfactory explanation for their former use; a few experts thought they were amulets or game figures. *But Schmandt-Besserat [cf. 1986, p. 34-35] noticed that the shape of many tokens matched with the form of archaic signs on tablets.* For example, *a disk with a cross,* can be found among the tokens as well as among the signs on clay tablets where it became a circle with cross enclosed. But this ideograph is traceable to later writings and *stands for "sheep"*; similarly, an ovoid with circular incision stands for a "jar of oil", a triangle with five incised lines means "metal (silver?)." The cone and the sphere stand for small and large measures of grain respectively; a cylinder may be interpreted as "one animal (sheep or goat?)" while a disk refers most likely to a "flock of animals probably half a score (i.e. ten)." But let us listen to Schmandt-Besserat herself:

Exhibit 2

2. **Complex clay tokens**

"About 200 spherical clay envelopes (including fragments) have been recovered in an area extending from Palestine to Iran, including Saudi Arabia. The seals impressed upon their surface indicate their formal character, and it seems clear that the tokens they contain stood for goods and stated liabilities. The envelopes would have remained of esoteric interest but for the discovery of their relationship to the invention of writing. Indeed, their evolution illustrates no less than the transition between an archaic abacus and writing according to the following sequence: (1) the invention of envelopes to hold tokens of specific transactions; (2) the impression of markings on the surface of the envelopes to indicate the shape and number of tokens included inside; (3) the collapse of the envelopes into clay balls or tablets bearing impressed signs; and (4) the elaboration of the impressed signs into incised pictographs.

The study of the envelopes therefore provides new insights into the origins of writing. It makes clear the process of its emergence from an archaic recording system based on tokens and throws light upon the fortuitous nature of its invention. It demonstrates that the cradle of writing was not confined to Mesopotamia but extended to the west as far as the upper Euphrates valley in Syria and to Elam at the east. The date of the events can be pinpointed to the Uruk IV period of 3200-3100 BC'' [Schmandt-Besserat, 1980, p. 385].

On the basis of this evidence few experts will doubt that the precursor of writing was the representation of commodities by means of clay symbols, not all of which were miniature models but *many were abstract shapes the meaning of which was determined by convention.* But what kind of messages did these symbols convey?

Data Processing and Accounting in Prehistoric Times

The *plain* clay tokens are dating from ca. 8000 B.C. onwards and were discovered among village finds (and later temple finds) unearthed in the Fertile Crescent of the Middle East.[5] These tokens were sometimes *enclosed in a "clay envelope"* (hollow clay ball some 10 cm in diameter, the surface of which bore markings — which in turn are among the first

---

[5]The first plain tokens (around 8000 B.C.) were extracted from the remains of "round hut compounds" on many archeological sites of the Fertile Crescent — typical sites: Tell Mureybet and Tell Aswad in Syria, as well as Tepe Asiab and Ganj Dareh Tepe in Iran. By the seventh millennium B.C. simple tokens were also used in an area reaching from present Turkey to Israel.

The proportion of perforated tokens varies according to sites. At Uruk, only 46% are perforated but at other sites, such as Habuba Kabira in Syria, up to 80% of the tokens have a hole.

evidence of writing — indicating the content for quick recognition, and seem to represent one of the earliest systematic accounting systems. One or several specimen from Uruk, for example, yielded the following tokens which Schmandt-Besserat could match to the corresponding commodities as shown below (adapted from Schmandt-Besserat 1983, p. 120):

Exhibit 3

3. Clay envelope (showing seal on surface) with five clay spheres.

3 incised ovoids	=	3 jars of oil
1 cylinder	=	1 animal (sheep or goat)
9 tetrahedrons	=	9 units of services
3 trussed ducks[6]	=	3 trussed ducks
5 ovoids	=	5 ?
4 parabolas	=	4 ?
1 triangle	=	1 small measure of grain?
26 spheres	=	26 bariga of grain[7]

---

[6]"Trussed ducks" on the left hand side refers to small clay tokens resembling trussed ducks, while the same expression on the right hand side refers to the slaughtered animals, similar to those in the supermarket.

[7]A *bariga* is a (larger) unit of measure used in Sumer — perhaps equivalent to the English "bushel."

It is not difficult to recognize that each of these eight lines represents a different *commodity account* identified by a specific shape of concrete tokens — just as businessmen give different names to different accounts, so the inhabitants of ancient Mesopotamia assigned *different shapes* (or tokens of different shapes) to different commodity accounts. Thus the singularity of "token accounting" lies in the multiplicity of shapes given to easily maleable clay tokens. Although these simple and concrete tokens were first associated with village life and agriculture, later on these "accounts" were kept (often together and even mixed with collections of the more sophisticated abstract tokens) by priests and temple administrators, so that the various shapes did not easily change their meaning — the shapes were conventionalized and seem to have kept their meaning for thousands of years. An *envelope* of tokens probably functioned as *a personal account about a steward or debtor* indicating the equity invested in such a person; but simultaneously it was an inventory list detailing this investment. Not always did one token stand for a single piece of commodity, sometimes it represented a specific measure of grain or a jar of oil, etc. Yet those units were only loosely standardized and should not be interpreted in any mathematical sense. But it is crucial to note that before 3,200 B.C. there is still no evidence that those concrete tokens represent numerals. At this stage, counting *in the abstract sense*, as we know it today, had not yet

Exhibit 4

4. **Clay envelope (showing traces of seal as well as impressions of hardened tokens) with tokens.**

emerged.[8] Thus it is correct to say thet *accounting preceded abstract counting.*

Complex Tokens

Complex tokens are distinguished from plain tokens by *a greater variety of token shapes, by markings on those tokens* (incisions, punctations or appliqué coils, and pellets added to the token surface), *by a perforation of those tokens for the purpose of stringing them and sealing them together* (instead of putting them into a clay envelope), and, above all, *by their more abstract usage.*[9] The term "abstract token" might be confusing

Exhibit 5

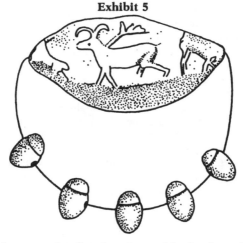

5. **Sketched reconstruction of a string aggregate (showing clay seal on top and five perforated ovoid tokens on string) — designed by Ellen Simmons.**

---

[8]The *crucial step* from token counting to a numerical system is best described by Bertrand Russell [1919/60, p. 3] who points out that "it must have taken ages to discover that a brace of pheasants and a couple of days were both instances of the number two."

[9]Whereas the *plain or concrete tokens* had plain unmarked surfaces and came in a limited number of simple geometric shapes (flat and lenticular disks, cones, tetrahedrons, cylinders and occasionally commodity and animal shapes), *the later complex or abstract tokens (closely tied to Sumerian temple institutions) bore marks on their surface* and came in a much greater number of shapes (spheres, disks, cones, tetrahedrons, biconoids, ovoids, cylinders, bent coils, triangles, parabolas, rectangles, rhomboids, container, animal and other shapes). Each shape and marking had a well specified meaning. Typical objects of reference of a token were: a measure of grain, a jar of oil, a fleece of wool, or even a pot of beer. The *cone* and *sphere* were usually *used for grain.* They correspond to the Sumerian *ban* and *bariga* which find their analogy in the English peck and bushel.

because those complex tokens are still concrete clay objects, but *now they are used in a way that approaches numerals in the abstract sense.* Thus the term "abstract" does not refer to the token itself but to its use. But just as in the case of clay envelopes, those sealed string collections are equivalent to personal accounts about stewards and debtors, and simultaneously lists of inventories.

The Input-Output Principle: From Ancient Mesopotamia to the 20th Century

We have seen that by 3200 B.C. two kinds of accounting techniques were employed, often simultaneously. The first consisted in keeping plain tokens of different shapes in a marked and sealed clay envelope, the other in keeping an even greater variety of complex (incised), perforated tokens on a sealed string. There is sufficient evidence indicating that the plain tokens referred to such assets as grain and cattle while the complex tokens referred to services and manufactured goods. *This separation resembles the distinction between cash items* (including receivables, payables, etc.) *and non-cash items* (inventories, equipment, land, etc.) in double entry accounting of the Italian Renaissance. And since grain and cattle were the payment units or "cash items" of ancient Mesopotamia, the parallel is all the more striking.

Each kind of token shape, whether plain or complex, can be interpreted as a type of account, and the number of tokens (in a clay envelope or on a string) of a particular shape represents the quantity of pertinent items. Then all tokens together (of different shapes in a particular envelope or on a string) represent an *equity* loosely aggregated by an envelope or string (instead of the highly abstract aggregation attainable by monetary values). This may seem primitive, yet *it spared the Sumerian scribe the valuation problem*, which not only plagues modern accountants but also removed accounting representation one further step from objective reality, creating subjectivity and adding ambiguity. Thus the "aggregate" or superaccount represented by a clay envelope or a collection of tokens on a string, is not too much different from a balance sheet. It certainly had a *dual* significance: in its details, it represented the individual assets, in its totality it represented an equity.

But what was the entity behind this equity? Since these "aggregates" were most frequently (but not exclusively) found in former temple grounds (often a great number of such envelopes and string systems were stored in a single temple), the

29

entity usually was a temple or, less frequently, an individual person, family, or other small social group. There is archeological evidence that temples levied taxes possibly on the basis of farming out temple assets to individual persons (debtors or stewards). Thus the entity was (at least by 3200 B.C.) in most cases *a temple institution,* and the "debtor" probably was a particular person. But to determine the entire equity of such a temple government one would have had to further aggregate all the envelopes and string aggregates within a temple precinct — but there may not have been any need for doing this since the main purpose of those accounting systems was the monitoring of the obligations and levies from individual stewards and tax payers. Such a system also lends itself to recording the actual payments in kind by the debtor — archeologists have, indeed, repeatedly emphasized the debt-nature of such a token aggregate and of many clay tablets of a later age. It is possible even that the tokens or token aggregates were handed over as receipts to the debtor or donor by the temple administrator once the former's debt was "paid" or a donation was made. But whatever the individual practices and techniques may have been, there can be little doubt that those ancient people moved clay tokens from one place to another in strict correspondence with the transfer of commodities and debt relations.

A Duality Principle

This means, first of all, that *those ancient people of the Middle East had record keeping systems, the basic logical structure of which was virtually identical with that of modern double entry.*[10] *One might reply that the transfer of ordinary goods, from one person to another, already possessed this logical structure which we call the input-output or duality principle.* This is perfectly correct, but *the ingenious stroke was to transfer this idea or principle from actual commodities by a one-to-one correspondence to a conceptual system of representation.* Once this crucial

---

[10]For some thirty years I have tried to make clear to accountants that the crucial event in accounting is not double entry — which, after all, is a mere technique — but *the logic structure* behind it [Mattessich 1957/82, 1964, 1987]. A set-theoretical analysis of this "flow" or "input-output" structure in terms of ownership and debt relations is found in Appendix A of Mattessich [1964, pp. 448-465]. I have also demonstrated that this structure can manifest itself in matrices, net works, vectors, algebraic equations, etc. Now we have evidence that this logic structure was already present in record keeping systems some 10,000 years ago.

fact of the *input-output* or *duality* principle has been established, the question whether the ancient Sumerians or any other tribe used (more than five thousand years ago) a *double entry system*, is of secondary importance.

However, a good case can be made that even *double entry (in the literal sense* of the word) *emerged as early as 3200 B.C.* From this time stem the earliest clay envelopes (bullae) that bear on their surface the impressions of the tokens contained inside. Putting those tokens into an envelope undoubtedly meant the recording of quantities of various assets, or what we today would call "making debit entries." But apart from this were two further needs: (1) to reveal from outside the hidden content of the envelope, and (2) to reveal at a glance the entire equity represented by the envelope — as far as such an aggregation is possible without a common denominator. By sheer coincidence both of these functions could be fulfilled by a single act, namely by impressing the hardened tokens into the surface of the softer clay envelope. If this interpretation is correct, then those "mirror impressions" can be regarded as genuine counter-entries (in this case, credit entries) on the equity side of such an accounting system — since each token inside the envelope represents an asset, and each impression outside is part of the total equity.

Considering that this not only happened more than five thousand years ago, before writing and abstract counting was invented, the long tradition of accounting must either inspire some awe or reinforce the view that accounting is a *dusty* discipline indeed — one that literally arose out of the clay or dust of the earth. But there are at least two further important aspects to be discussed, both of which have philosophic implications.

The Correspondence Theory of Representation

The importance of Ludwig Wittgenstein for the philosophy of science as well as for every individual science lies in his enduring concern with *questions of representation*: How can language represent reality? What makes it possible for a combination of words to represent a fact? How is it that a sentence can *say* that such-and-such is the case?

In his first major work, the *Tractatus Logico-Philosophicus*, Wittgenstein [1922] developed his "picture theory" which regards a sentence as a picture (i.e. a model of reality) in the following sense: How is it possible that confronted *for the first time* with a sentence (composed of familiar words), we under-

31

stand this sentence without any explanation? Although a sentence cannot *say* its meaning (it is only capable of saying that so-and-so is the case), it can *show* its meaning.[11] And if it can show this, then it must be some kind of picture of reality. Even more critical is that in the *Tractatus* Wittgenstein asserts that the relation between the elementary or atomic parts of a *true* sentence must be in one-to-one correspondence with the objects and constituents of a fact, i.e. with reality — and it is, above all, this "logical atomism" together with its "correspondence theory of truth" which he abandons in his later philosophy.[12] Because if

> challenged to explain *why* we must suppose that language is related to the world in that particular way, he was — on his own confession — in no position to give any literal reply ... Propositions were capable of modeling and, so, describing reality; but they could not simultaneously describe *how* they described it, without becoming selfreferential and consequently meaningless" [Janik and Toulmin, 1973, pp. 189-190].

Thus the *Tractatus* has the merit of *revealing the limitations* of propositional language. It shows that *logic* as well as *ethics* are transcendental. The *Tractatus* must not be misinterpreted to be a positivistic work: "Positivism holds — and this is its essence — that what we can speak about is all that matters in life. *Whereas Wittgenstein passionately believes that all that really matters in human life is precisely what, in his view, we must be silent about*" [Engleman, 1967, p. 97].

Wittgenstein's second major work, *The Philosophical Investigations* (published posthumously in 1953) at least as influential as the *Tractatus*, constitutes a rejection of some of his major previous thoughts, but it also is a continuation of his

---

[11]"In a letter to Russell, Wittgenstein remarked that his "main contention" was this distinction between what can be said in propositions — i.e. in language — and what cannot be said but can only be shown. This he said, was "the cardinal problem of philosophy" Malcolm [1967, p. 330].

[12]With reference to the *important* problem of Wittgenstein's *connecting of elementary or atomic propositions with complex propositions*, [Hintika, 1987, p. 30] offers the following crucial insight: "In the *Tractatus*, Wittgenstein used the truth function theory to extend his picturing idea from atomic propositions to all complex ones. In 1928-29 he gave up his belief that truth-function theory could serve as such a bridge. Henceforth the same role had to be played by suitable human activities ("calculi", later "language games"). The nature of these activities was the main problem of his later philosophy."

earlier philosophic quest. Here the notion of "language games" and the importance of linguistic *conventions* supersede the "picture theory." From now on the *meaning* of a sentence is not derived from the picture property but from the *use and application* of the sentence. Wittgenstein's second philosophy is no longer limited to the natural sciences and rejects the notion that every form (structure) of a proposition can be anticipated as a new combination of simple objects.[13] On the contrary, new language games are possible and embody new "forms of living" (Lebensformen). The meaning of a name is not the object it pertains to; and naming is not prior to the meaning of a sentence because before we know what a name stands for, we must already have mastered the pertinent language game.

> So, from now on, Wittgenstein focused his attention instead on *language as behaviour*: concentrating his expressions, on the *language games* within which those rules are operative, and on the broad *forms of life* which ultimately give those language games their significance. The heart of the "transcendental" problem thus ceased (for Wittgenstein) to lie in the formal character of linguistic representations; instead, it became an element in "the natural history of man" [Janik and Toulmin, 1973, p. 223].

The accounting systems of the Sumerians and other ancient peoples are obviously not comprehensive or complete language systems (in the ordinary sense), and thus cannot offer any evidence for or against the validity of logical atomism and the correspondence theory of truth. But they are something like specialized and limited language systems or, more precisely, *representational systems* for the purpose of giving account of an entity's wealth and its flow. And as such they might provide evidence for the *usefulness* of the *correspondence theory of representation*. Not only did every piece of commercial reality (a measure of grain, a ewe or ram, a jar of oil or a weight of silver)

---

[13]"The *Tractatus* held that the ultimate elements of language are names that designate simple objects. In the *Investigations* it is argued that the words "simple" and "complex" have no *absolute* meaning." In the Tractatus the existence of simple objects was conceived as following from the requirement that the sense of sentences is *definite*. In the *Investigations* this requirement is regarded as another philosophical illusion. We have imagined an "ideal" of languages that will not satisfy actual needs . . . Wittgenstein denied that we always understand a sentence . . . sentences have sense only in special circumstances; in other circumstances we do not understand them . . . The view of the *Tractatus* is entirely different [Malcolm, 1967, pp. 335-336].

correspond to a specific token, but also such *relations*, as transfer, property rights, and debt claims, were represented by
proper correspondences in this accounting system (through the
location of certain tokens in a particular aggregate).[14] It does
not matter that this system itself consisted of relatively concrete objects (like clay cylinders, cones, etc.) instead of more
abstract, written symbols; on the contrary this intermediary
step reveals to us the evolution of a conceptual system — it not
only demonstrates that *abstraction is a matter of degree* but also
how more abstract representational systems evolved from less
abstract ones. Above all, the archeological evidence shows that
the first systematic representational system was based on a
correspondence notion. The crucial thing is that *input-output
relations apply not only to the actual transfer of commodities but
also to their representations.* Because for the purpose of giving
account of those transfers of commodities, property claims, and
their results, clay tokens were removed from one place and put
into another.

This archeological evidence shows two things: (1) that the
precursor of written language was a system of representation
that exploited the one-to-one correspondence between segments of reality and certain more or less abstract symbols, and
(2) that such a one-to-one correspondence proved useful for
almost five thousand years as a major element of what was
probably the only systematic representational system available
to early agricultural communities as well as to the first phase
of urban culture. With this statement we do *not* negate the
objections raised against logical atomism, but we suggest that
in certain representations situations — particular in those with
a manageable range and clearly defined concepts — there is a
place for the correspondence theory.

---

[14]One might argue that the much older paleolithic cave paintings and
miniature art constitute earlier evidence for a correspondence theory of representation. But in these caves only objects (e.g. animals and hunters) are
clearly represented while the relationships are, at best, merely implied. Certainly, the *systematics* necessary for a representational system, and the evidence afforded by the clay envelopes and string aggregates of the token
accounting systems, is nowhere found in paleolithic art. In other words,
paleotithic art represented mainly objects while neolithic record keeping
represented *objects* as well as *facts* in Wittgenstein's sense (i.e. relations
between objects). However, this hypothesis may founder if Margulis and
Sagan's [1986, p. 222] *guess* is correct that "hunter-gatherers were sketching
maps and plotting the movement of planets and stars as early as 40,000 years
ago."

Janik and Toulmin [1973] claim that the historical root of Wittgenstein's concern for language and "pictorial" representation lies less in Russell's influence than in Wittgenstein's Viennese background:

> Far from originating in Wittgenstein's *Tractatus*, as we shall see, the idea of regarding language, symbolism and media of expression of all kinds as giving us "representations" (*Darstellungen*) or "pictures" (*Bilder*) had by 1910 become a commonplace in all fields of Viennese cultural debate. Among scientists this notion had been in circulation at least since the time of Hertz, who had characterized physical theories as providing just such a *Bild* or *Darstellung* of natural phenomena [footnote omitted]. At the other extreme, it was equally familiar among artists and musicians; Arnold Schönberg, for instance, wrote an essay on musical thoughts, with the title *Der Musikalische Gedanke und die Logik, Technik, und Kunst seiner Darstellung* [footnote omitted]. By the time Wittgenstein came to the scene, this debate had been going on for some fifteen or twenty years in the drawing rooms of Vienna..." [Janik and Toulmin, 1973, p.31].

These authors also refer to the influence which the writings of the renowned physicist Heinrich R. Hertz [1894] — who was trying to present a "picture theory" as a system of mathematical models — had on Wittgenstein:

> We form for ourselves images or symbols of external objects; and the form which we give them is such that the necessary consequence of the images in thought are always the images of the necessary consequence in nature of the things pictured. In order that this requirement may be satisfied, there must be a certain conformity between nature and our thought. Experience teaches us that the requirement can be satisfied, and hence that such a conformity does in fact exist. When from our accumulated previous experience we have once succeeded in deducing images of the desired nature, we can then in a short time develop by means of them, as by means of models, the consequences which in the external world only arise in a comparatively long time, or as the result of our own interposition. We are thus enabled to be in advance of the facts, and to decide as to present affairs in accordance with the insight so obtained. The images which we here speak of are our

35

conceptions of things. With the things themselves they are in conformity in one important respect, namely, in satisfying the above-mentioned requirement. For our purpose it is not necessary that they should be in conformity with the things in any other respect whatever [Hertz, 1899, pp. 1-2].

It seems that Hertz too had in mind a correspondence theory, but limited to mathematics in relation to the essential features of physics. Wittgenstein, on the other hand was ambitious enough in his *Tractatus* to expand this idea to language in general as well as to all aspects of factual reality (i.e. excluding value judgments). And this venture had to fail as the emergence of Wittgenstein's [1953] second philosophy clearly showed [Mattessich, 1978, pp. 95-97]. In other words the correspondence theory of representation may be defensible only when applied to certain precisely defined languages in correspondence with a limited aspect of reality (physical phenomena, certain economic and accounting phenomena, etc.).

Early Accounting Systems as Precursor of Counting, Writing and Model Building

Counting seems to have emerged in three different stages — counting by (1) one-to-one matching of *unspecialized* tokens like pebbles, sticks, etc., (2) by *specialized* tokens (abstract symbols as well as those with morphological similarities to the objects represented), and (3) counting with genuine numerals, abstracted from any token symbols [Schmandt-Besserat, 1983 and 1986a]. Only the last stage is counting in the proper or modern, abstract sense; it seems to have emerged around 3200 B.C., simultaneously with writing. This is no coincidence because the evidence is strong that both activities arose from the need to mark the surface of the clay envelopes in such a way that the number and kinds of tokens contained in them could easily be discerned. This was done by impressing each token contained on the soft clay surface (the precursor of cuneiform writing), but often not enough space may have been on the surface, so a specific shape may have been combined with a purely numerical sign (e.g. a number of dots, the first truly abstract numerals).

But those early accounting systems reveal more, something of special interest to philosophers pondering over Wittgenstein's ideas. Those token systems show that the one-to-one correspondence between the tokens (including their position in a specific envelope or on a string aggregate) and the pertinent economic facts, are *not* logic relations that can be syntactically defined,[15] but are *semantic relations to be "shown" by usage.* But this might hold only when dealing with "abstract token shapes." Where tokens with morphological similarities to the commodities are involved, one might be able to argue that the link between the written language and reality is a geometric, hence logical-mathematical relation.

In spite of the fact that this still leaves a "semantic gap" between written and spoken language, it hints at the possibility that there may be an evolutionary link between logic (in the narrow sense of syntactics) and semantics — not only on the theoretical but also on the practical level. This difference between syntactics and semantics might come close to the distinction between "stating" and "showing." And the connection between the two asumes particular importance in our modern world of video and computer technology. Because the latter has acquired the ability to *state* or *describe* certain aspects of reality by means of a logical sequence of magnetized dots (*digital* representation) which in turn are further processed to *show* this reality in form of sounds and more or less genuine pictures (*analogue* representation).

To master their environment and to manipulate it for the satisfaction of their own needs, biological organisms have evolved a great variety of reaction mechanisms. In the higher animals the most important one is the creation of ideas or mental images. This is our window to the world, which, however, requires certain intermediaries. These are *encoding/ decoding* systems in the form of the internal neuronal language system and various external language systems. Whether it is a representation through neurons, or the prehistoric representation of reality through tokens, or modern video-computer imagery, in all cases the semantic gap between an *abstract* representation (e.g. a sequence of magnetic dots) and the *more concrete* representation (a television picture) is bridged by some kind of language code. Such a code may be purely syntactical, but usually incorporates a system of conventions ("usages") which go beyond mere logical relations. But whether the latter are too complex or ambiguous for scientific purposes or whether it is for any other reason, the fact is that modern semantics fashioned itself to a considerable extent on

---

[15]In Wittgenstein's terminology: "said", "stated" or "described" *in contrast* to "shown". But possibly my interpretation of those words somewhat differs from that of Wittgenstein.

the syntax of logic which, however, should not blur the difference between the two.

Two Views

Furthermore we have seen that both, the prehistoric recording systems as well as the modern video and computer systems, demonstrate that the *representational view* (of the early Wittgenstein) and the *functional view* (of the later Wittgenstein) are compatible and do not need to exclude each other. Prehistoric accounting systems reveal the logical, indeed set-theoretical, structure inherent in certain economic aspects of reality. The clay envelopes and string aggregates possess the structure of sets — or precisely sets of sets, because the super-set of the entire aggregate can be understood as containing subsets, each represented by a different token shape. Hence the relations involved are those of "being a *subset* of"($\subset$), "being an *element* of" ($\in$)and a "transaction" (an input-output vector). And the notorious *duality* of accounting arises out of the dual interpretation of a set as a collection of elements (the input) on one side, and as a kind of totality (the output), on the other. And a deeper analysis reveals that this duality, in turn, is rooted in a physical input-output dichotomy manifesting a *conservation principle*: the giving account of a certain input in terms of its output in such economic transactions as the transfer of commodities from one "place" to another, be it for the purpose of buying, lending, repaying, manufacturing, selling, etc.

My Answer to Wittgenstein

Based on the preceding analysis, let me draw my conclusions:

First, how can we characterize the *difference* between "saying" and "showing"? And is there a link between the two? To simply state that sentences *say*, while pictures *show*, will not do. Probing into the prehistory and early history of writing has hopefully lifted some fog. Token accounting as well as cuneiform writing, hieroglyphs, offer many examples of various steps by which *morphological tokens* (i.e. those with similarity to its referent) and *pictographs* (both of which seem "to show") developed into abstract tokens and ideographs (both of which seem "to say"). And now we may raise two questions: (1) At what stage did a symbol lose its ability "to show"? And (2) at what stage did it gain the ability "to say"?

The first question is relatively easy to answer: As soon as the *structural similarity* between a symbol and its referent gets lost, it can no longer "show" — in this morphology and its loss lies *the difference* between "showing" and "saying." And this loss usually occurs at a fairly early stage in the development of a sign.

Even more important, and perhaps more difficult to answer, is the second question. My personal reply is this: morphological tokens and pictographs do not only "show", they also "say" (Marshall McLuhan may have said: "pictographs *are* the message"); or more formally: *from its earliest development on such symbols are endowed with the power to say.*[16] Thus the *morphological tokens and pictographs not only describe structures, they themselves are similar structures.* Yet in subsequent steps of development — when these morphological similarities have vanished — how can those now abstract tokens or signs (in conjunction with some relations: e.g. placing a token into a specific receptacle) continue to describe factual entities and relations? The evolution of those tokens and linguistic signs clearly shows that this "miracle" is made possible through the previously established *associations* between each abstract sign and the corresponding morphological token or pictograph which in turn is structurally related to the pertinent empirical object or fact. On a higher or later level this crucial *association* is established by conventions — which might explain why the later Wittgenstein put so much emphasis on linguistic conventions.

Our facit is that morphological tokens and pictographs are a common denominator for "showing" and "saying" — those symbols might be the *missing link* between those two activities. And because there exists such a connection, it might be possible that aggregates of machines like a complete video system is capable of transforming something that shows into something that says, and *vice versa*.

And finally, my answer to Wittgenstein's *perennial* question is that: the representation of reality by means of signs is possible because language itself is a double-sided *Janus-faced* creation — not unlike our mind/brain system. *Language is*

---

[16]This seems to be in disagreement with Wittgenstein's [1922 item 4.1212] "what *can* be shown, *cannot* be said" and I wonder whether this is due to a difference in our notions of "showing" and "saying" or in some misunderstanding.

capable of conveying ideas, yet it is deeply rooted in such physical realities as vibrations of air, tokens and tablets of clay, ink on papyrus or paper, magnetized dots on plastic tapes, etc. Both, language and the mind/brain system, belong to the *realm of concepts and forms* as well as to the *realm of matter and energy.* Everyday languages as well as scientific and technical languages are possible for the same reason that makes our genetic, our neuronal and our hormonal language systems possible. Our social languages are certainly not our own original inventions, they are merely copies or re-inventions of nature's work; and it seems that all "natural" as well as "social" languages are a manifestation of *nature's basic duality* of conceptualization and legislation, on one side, and execution and material manifestation on the other.

REFERENCES

Diringer, D., *The Alphabet*, Vol. 1, 3rd ed., London: Hutchison, 1964.

Engelman, P., *Letters from Ludwig Wittgenstein, With a Memoir*, B. F. McGuinness, (ed.), transl. by L. Furtmüller, Oxford: Basil Blackwell, 1967.

Falkenstein, A., *Archaische Texte aus Uruk, Ausgrabungen der Deutschen Forschungsgemeinschaft in Uruk-Warka*, Berlin: Deutsche Forschungsgemeinschaft, 1936.

_____. *Keilschriftforschung und Alte Geschichte Vorderasiens*, Leiden: E. J. Brill, 1964.

Hawkes, J., (ed.), *The World of the Past*, Vol. 1, New York: Simon and Schuster, 1963.

Hertz, H. R., *Gesammelte Werke*, 3 Vols., Leipzig: J. A. Barth, 1894.

_____. *The Principles of Mechanics Presented in a New Form*, transl. by D. E. Jones and J. W. Wallery, London: MacMillan Co., 1899.

Hintikka, Jaakko, "Ludwig Wittgenstein: Half-Truths and One-and-a-half Truths." *Philosophy of Law, Politics, and Society – Abstracts*, 12th International Wittgenstein Symposium, Kirchberg: 1987, pp. 30-31.

Janik, A. and S. Toulmin, *Wittgenstein's Vienna*. New York: Simon and Schuster, 1973.

Jasmin, S. A. and J. Oates, "Early Tokens and Tablets in Mesopotamia: New Information from Tell Abada and Tell Brak." *World Archeology* (February 1986), pp. 348-362.

Malcolm, N., "Wittgenstein, Ludwig Joseph Johann." *Encyclopedia of Philosophy*, Vol. 8, Paul Edwards (ed.), New York: MacMillan Co. and The Free Press, 1967, pp. 327-340.

Mallowan, M. E. L., "The Birth of Written History" in Pigott (1961), pp. 65-96.

Mattessich, R., "Towards a General and Axiomatic Foundation of Accountancy — With an Introduction to the Matrix Formulation of Accounting Systems." *Accounting Research* (today: *Journal of Accounting and Business Research*) Vol. 8, No. 4 (October 1957), pp. 328-55. Reprinted in *The Accounting Postulate and Principles Controversy of the 1960's*, S. A. Zeff (ed.), New York: Garland, 1982.

_____. *Accounting and Analytical Methods – Measurement and Projection of Income and Wealth in the Micro- and Macro-Economy*. Homewood, Ill.: Richard D. Irwin, 1964.

——————. *Instrumental Reasoning and Systems Methodology – An Epistemology of the Applied and Social Sciences*, Dordrecht-Holland: D. Reidel Publishing Co., 1978.

——————. "An Applied Scientist's Search for a Methodological Framework" in *Logic, Philosophy of Science and Epistemology – Proceedings of the 11th International Wittgenstein Symposium ed. by Paul Weingartner and Gerhard Schurz, Vienna: Hölder-Pichler-Tempskey, 1987* pp. 243-262.

Margulis, L., and D. Sagan, *Microcosm – Four Billion Years of Evolution from Our Microbial Ancestors*, New York: Simon and Schuster, 1986.

Pigott, S. (ed.), *The Dawn of Mankind*, New York: McGraw-Hill Co., 1961.

Russell, B., *Introduction to Mathematical Philosophy*. London: George Allen and Unwin, 1919, 10th ed. 1960.

Schmandt-Besserat, Denise. "The Earliest Precursor of Writing." *Scientific American*, Vol. 238, No. 6 (1978), pp. 50-58.

——————. "The Envelopes that Bear the First Writing." *Technology and Culture*, Vol. 21, No. 3 (1980), pp. 357-385.

——————. "Tablets and Tokens: A Re-examination of the So-called 'Numerical Tablets'." *Visible Language*, Vol. 15 (1981), pp. 321-344.

——————. "Decipherment of the Earliest Tablets." *Science*, Vol. 211 (1981a), pp. 283-285.

——————. "Tokens and Counting." *Biblical Archeologist*, (Spring 1983), pp. 117-120.

——————. "The Emergence of Recording." *American Anthropologist*, Vol. 84 (1984), pp. 871-878.

——————. "Before Numerals". *Visible Language*, Vol. 15, No. 1 (1984), pp. 48-59.

——————. "The Origins of Writing — An Archeologist's Perspective." *Written Communication*, Vol. 3, No. 1 (January 1986), pp. 31-45.

——————. "The Precursor to Numerals and Writing." *Archeology*, (Nov./Dec. 1986a), pp. 32-38.

Vallat, F., "The Most Ancient Script of Iran: The Current Situation." *World Archeology* (February 1986), pp. 335-347.

Wittgenstein, L., *Tractatus Logico-Philosophicus*. London: Routledge and Kegan Paul, 1922.

——————. *Philosophical Investigations* ed. by G. H. von Wright and G. E. M. Anscombe, Oxford: Basil Blackwell, 1953.

OTHER REFERENCES

The illustrations of Clay Tokens and Token Accounting Systems are from Susa, Iran, ca. 3350-3200 B.C. (courtesy Musée du Louvre, Department des Antiqués Orientales).

CHAPTER 3

Counting, Accounting, and the Input-Output Principle

Recent Archeological Evidence Revising Our View on the Evolution of Early Record Keeping

Counting, Accounting, and the Input-Output Principle: Recent Archeological Evidence Revising Our View on the Evolution of Early Record Keeping

Richard Mattessich
University of British Columbia (Emeritus)

Abstract: Apart from a concise recapitulation of Schmandt-Besserat's archeological research on counting and token accounting (ca. 8000 to 3000 B.C.), this paper offers a pertinent interpretation from an accountant's point of view. It formulates and examines the input-output principle with regard to physical and social transfers, as well as the duality structure and double recording of token accounting. Particular emphasis is put on the logical form of transactions, and the difference between economic transactions, as empirical manifestations, versus accounting transactions, as their conceptual representations. Finally, the principle of conservation (symmetry) as applied to accounting is discussed.*

DID ACCOUNTING PRECEDE ABSTRACT COUNTING?

Historians of mathematics accept the hypothesis that the evolution of "counting" (in the broadest sense) proceeded in several distinct stages.[1] Recent archeological research in Middle Eastern writing and counting by Schmandt-Besserat [1980, 1983, 1984] yields evidence to

---

*Financial support for this project by the Social Science and Humanities Research Council of Canada, and the valuable correspondence with and many suggestions from, Professor Denise Schmandt-Besserat are gratefully acknowledged. This article is an accounting interpretation of Schmandt-Besserat's [1977, 1978, 1980, 1981, 1981a, 1982, 1984, 1986, 1986a] archeological research and is partly based on Mattessich [1987, 1988, 1989]. In spite of some recapitulation and overlapping with those papers, this article contains new insights and conjectures relevant to the history and foundations of accounting; it has been chosen as "Best 1988 Paper" at the Annual Convention of the Canadian Academic Accounting Association in Windsor, Ontario.

[1] For a survey of prehistoric record keeping see also Schmandt-Besserat [1980, pp. 358-61] as well as Jasim and Oats [1986, p. 348]; for a somewhat different archeological interpretation see Vallat [1986, pp. 334-7], and Ifrah [1981/87]. For the history of counting, see Danzig [1959], E.E. Kramer [1970], and Flegg [1983].

support this and other hypotheses related to accounting. Following Schmandt-Besserat [1984] one characterizes three evolutionary stages— which may be called *counting by one-to-one matching, concrete counting,* and *abstract counting.*

COUNTING BY ONE-TO-ONE MATCHING

This involves *the creation of a one-to-one correspondence between a sign* (e.g., a pebble, a small stick or a curb on a bone,) *and a commodity*, like a goat, a measure of grain, or a coconut, *repeating the sign for every additional unit of this commodity.* Animal bones and antlers marked with notches excavated at Paleolithic and Mesolithic sites fall into this category. One of the earliest evidence, the famous "wolf bone," ca. 18 cm long, containing 55 notches, and found in Moravia in 1937 by Karl Absalom is "clear evidence that the tallying principle for [concrete] numbers goes back at least thirty thousand years" [Flegg, 1983, p. 42]. The Vedda tribe of Ceylon (Sri Lanka) seemed to have used a similar method until relatively recently. Its members, in using a series of small sticks, did not abstract those signs but merely pointed to the lot of them, saying: "that many." This means, for example, as many sticks you see here, as many coconuts should be on the pile yonder. One hardly dares to call such a primitive procedure "counting," but as *a method of accounting* (in the sense of accountability and record keeping) it is quite effective. Although *unaggregated* (or aggregated in a very primitive sense),[2] the series of signs enabled those tribesmen to account for the quantity of the pertinent goods by providing a fairly permanent record and check. Such sticks or pebbles are likely to have been used for many kinds of commodities and it is tempting to conjecture that this first stage of counting was the birth of abstract numbering. But the experts seem to deny this [cf. Schmandt-Besserat, 1984, p. 52]; although they admit that here some kind of abstraction manifests itself already, they point out that there is neither any indication of a set or quantified collection, nor is the object of this proto-abstraction a *numeral.*[3] They argue that

---

[2]I regard *aggregation as a matter of degree.* A collection of physical objects in a specific location (e.g., a pot or box) is probably the most primitive way of aggregation, while adding some numerals or monetary values is an abstract and more sophisticated way of aggregating.

[3]"*Numerals* are symbols to represent abstract numbers. Abstract means removed from concrete reality. *Abstract counting* refers to using number concepts abstracted from any particular collection. As a result 1,2,3,. . . are universally acceptable. Concrete counting, on the other hand, does not abstract numbers from the things counted. As a result, in *concrete counting* the number words that express the concepts "one," "two," "three," etc. differ according to whether, for instance, men, canoes, or trees are being counted. These different sets of number words, which change according to the category of item counted, are called *concrete numbers.*" Schmandt-Besserat [1984], p. 48.

those unaggregated or primitively aggregated signs were *case specific*, since only the persons performing or attending such a particular record keeping event were aware which commodity was actually matched. Even the next evolutionary step did not involve abstract numbers, but created a device capable of permanently identifying the commodity recorded by this one-to-one correspondence.

CONCRETE COUNTING BY TOKENS AND
SPECIFIC NUMBER WORDS

Simple Tokens (see Exhibit 1). We are here dealing with *special enumeration* through *concrete* tokens and *specific* number words. The most frequently cited example of this second stage stems from the eminent anthropologist Franz Boas [1889] who studied, among many other American Indian tribes, the Tsimshians of British Columbia. This tribe uses different, highly specific numberwords for different objects even when the same numeral is involved—more precisely, this language possesses *a set of seven words* for each of the first ten numbers (see Table 1). Yet this example reveals only a vestige of the second stage of numbering, as the Tsimshians also seem to have been in possession of abstract numbers and the corresponding general numberwords (see last column of Table 1). But as "it must have taken ages to discover that a brace of pheasants and a couple of days were both instances of the number two" [Russell, 1919/60, p. 3], the following example offers recent evidence of times when this crucial step of abstraction was not yet made.

Collections of *plain, concrete clay tokens of various shapes* (approx. 1 to 4 cm across) over 10,000 years old have been discovered among village finds (and later temple finds) unearthed in great numbers in the Fertile Crescent of the Middle East. Starting about 3250 B.C. these tokens were sometimes *enclosed in hollow clay balls* (some 10 cm in diameter—see Exhibit 2), which Legrain [1921] originally called "bulles sphériques" and which Schmandt-Besserat [1980, p. 359] prefers to address as *clay envelopes*.[4] On occasion the surface of these receptacles or "envelopes" bore markings—which in turn are among the first evidence of writing—indicating the content at a glance (Exhibit 3). These seem to be the earliest systematic accounting systems. Particularly striking is Schmandt-Besserat's presentation of such tokens from Uruk. She was able to match those tokens to the commodities to be represented in the following way [adapted from Schmandt-Besserat, 1983, p. 120]:

---

[4]It is suspected that before 3250 B.C. token receptacles of more perishable material were used.

Table 1
Number Words of the Tsimshians of British Columbia

Number	Men	Canoes	Long Objects	Flat Objects	Round Objects	Measures	Counting
1	k'al	k'amaet	k'awutskan	gak	g'erel	k'al	gyak
2	t'epqadal	g'alpeeltk	gaopskan	t'epqat	goupel	gulbel	t'epqat
3	gulal	galtskantk	galtskan	guant	gule	guleont	guant
4	tqalpqdal	tqalpqsk	tqaapskan	tqalpq	tqalpq	tqalpqalont	tqalpq
5	kcenecal	kctoonsk	k'etoentskan	kctonc	kctonc	kctonsilont	kctonc
6	k'aldal	k'altk	k'aoltskan	k'alt	k'alt	k'aldelont	k'alt
7	t'epqaldal	t'epqaltk	t'epqaltskan	t'epqalt	t'epqalt	t'epqaldelont	t'epqalt
8	yuktleadal	yuktaltk	ek'tlaedskan	yuktalt	yuktalt	yuktaldelont	guandalt
9	kctemacal	kctemack	kctemaetskan	kctemac	kctemac	kctemasilont	kctemac
10	kpal	gy'apsk	kpeetskan	gy'ap	kpeel	kpeont	gy'ap

The Tsimshians of British Columbia used these various number words according to whether they were counting men, canoes, long objects, flat objects, round objects or time, measures and any other item. The use of different numeration systems to count different items is called "concrete counting." Reproduced from Schmandt-Besserat [1984], p. 50.

Exhibit 1
Plain Clay Tokens

Exhibit 2

Clay Envelope (Showing Seal on Surface) with Five Clay Spheres

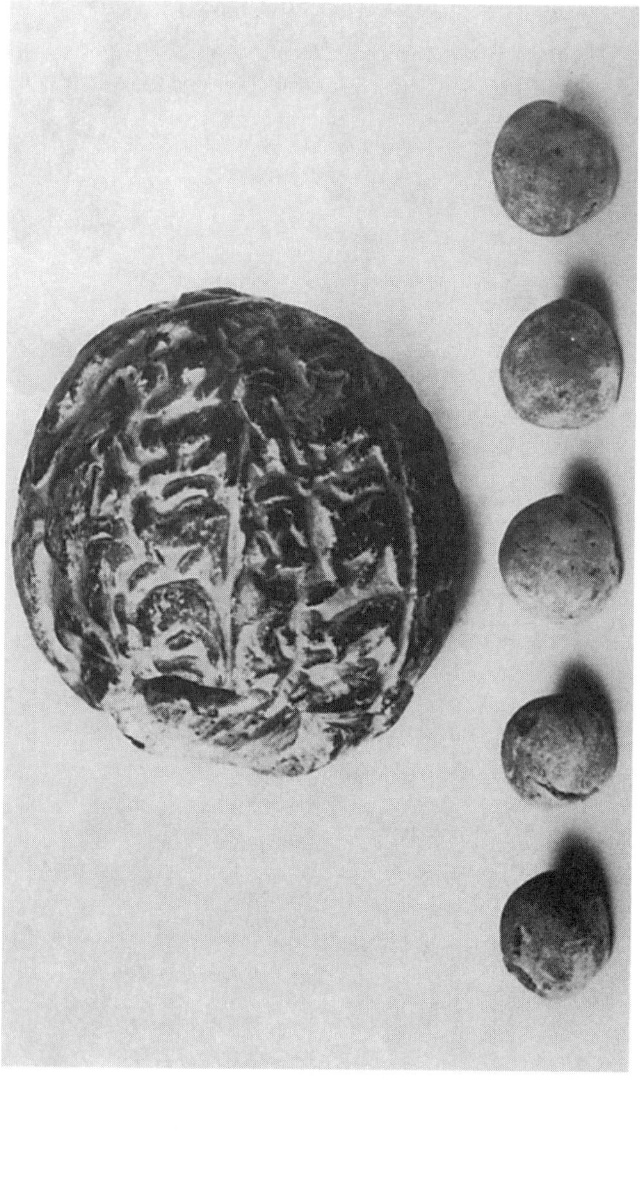

Exhibit 3
Clay Envelope (Showing Traces of Seal as Well as Impressions of Hardened Tokens) with Tokens

Exhibit 4
Complex Clay Tokens

Exhibit 5

Sketched Reconstruction of a String Aggregate (Showing Clay Seal on Top and Five Perforated Ovoid Tokens on String) Designed by Prof. Schmandt-Besserat

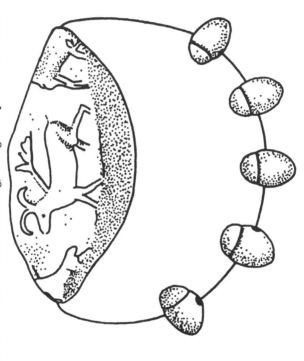

Tokens (Accounts)	Commodities
3 incised ovoids	= 3 jars of oil
1 cylinder	= 1 animal (sheep or goat)
9 tetrahedrons	= 9 units of services
3 shapes of trussed ducks	= 3 trussed ducks
5 ovoids	= 5 (still unidentified)
4 parabolas	= 4 (still unidentified)
1 triangle	= 1 small measure of grain?
26 spheres	= 26 bariga (larger measures) of grain

Thus every type of token is basically a specific type of *account*—what we discriminate by words or names, the ancient Sumerians discriminated by token shapes. Thus the main feature of "token accounting" is to be found in the diversity of shapes made possible by moldable clay that could be hardened by kiln fire thereby imparting greater permanence to the tokens.

A sphere with tokens was equivalent to *a personal account* representing that portion of the total assets (or equity) invested in a particular debtor but at the same time it constituted an inventory revealing further details. As each token stood for a single piece of a commodity, quantities of various kinds of goods could easily be tracked. But this primitive form of aggregation was limited by the *lack* of abstract numbers.

Complex Tokens (see Exhibit 4). These tokens offer *a greater diversity of shapes, various markings,* and *perforations for stringing them together*. This proliferation of shapes and markings of tokens indicates an increase in the number of goods accounted for. These changes, which occurred during the formation of the Sumerian city states show the correlation between the development of accounting and bureaucratic growth. It may be that the multiplication of tokens coincided with the imposition of mandatory dues to the state and the control it entails. The complex tokens enabled the keeping track of a larger number of different commodities in a more specific way; but like the plain ones, each complex token still represented one unit of a particular good or service. The clay receptacles, as well as the sealed string of tokens, are *both* corresponding to accounts about stewards or debtors, with accompanying lists of inventories. It is crucial to note, therefore, that before 3200 B.C. there is no evidence that either plain or complex tokens represent numerals. Counting *in the abstract sense*, as we know it today, had not yet emerged at this stage. And in this particular sense one may assert that *accounting preceded abstract counting*.

ABSTRACT COUNTING

Abstract numbers (numerals) seem to have emerged, simultaneous with writing, after 3200 B.C. in the Sumerian city states, soon after complex tokens came in use. The first evidence of the use of abstract numbers occurs on Sumerian clay tablets showing lists of goods. The signs indicating the items counted derived their shapes from tokens. However, instead of repeating the token two, three or four times to indicate two, three or four units of a product, the written sign was preceded by a numeral—a sign that expressed a number. These numerals denoting the concept of oneness, twoness, threeness, could be applied to the counting of jars of oil, as well as measures of grain or any other kind of goods. At this stage the concept of a number is no longer identified with a specific item counted, but assumes an abstract or Platonic existence of its own. This enabled the universal application of such *natural numbers* as 1, 2, 3, etc. to all kinds of countable objects. Abstract counting depends on several factors, not only on designating individual items, but also on identifying them with an ordered series of numbers, and being aware that the number assigned to the last item of the collection is identical to the total number counted—cf. the interesting article by Bower [1987] on "Calculating Apes."[5] The transition from the more concrete to the more abstract is illustrated by Smith [1951, p. 8] who lists examples in which primitive societies derived their number words from concrete enumerations frequently in use. He points out that the Nunes of the Southern Pacific counted with numbers that literally meant "one fruit, two fruits, three fruits," while in other situations the numbers meant "one grain, two grains, three grains," or "one stone, two stones, three stones."

After these preliminary considerations, we turn to the implications of this development. The logical structure of transactions and the various possibilities of their conceptual representation receive particular attention.

THE INPUT-OUTPUT PRINCIPLE: FROM ANCIENT MESOPOTAMIA TO THE TWENTIETH CENTURY

There exists evidence that the simple tokens represented grain, sheep and goats whereas the complex tokens represented labor and manufactured commodities.[6] *This suggests a similarity with the*

---

[5]See also Piaget's [1977, pp. 37-44] exposition on the "Logical nature of the whole number" and children's stages in attaining "general" or abstract categories [p. 41].

[6]"Despite the relative lateness in date of such envelopes, they predominantly held plain tokens and rarely complex ones, a fact which would argue for the distinctly different uses to which plain and complex tokens were normally put.

Whereas simple tokens were found in and refer to the commodities of agricultural communities, complex tokens not only arise in urban centers, but also quite clearly pertain to products of urban workshops. Moreover, as we shall see, complex tokens constitute a much more complicated accounting system by virtue of their varying shapes and the

distinction between cash items and noncash items in early Renaissance bookkeeping;[7] it is all the more striking as grain, sheep and goats were, indeed, the "cash" and payment units of the ancient Middle East.

ENTITIES, STEWARDSHIP AND DEBTOR RELATIONS

I have interpreted each type of token *shape* as *a type of account*, and the *number* of tokens (of a particular shape) contained in a clay envelope or on a string indicates *the quantity* of specific items. Consequently the sum total of the various tokens in a particular envelope or on a string stood for that part of his equity which a creditor lent to a debtor. Such a primitive system is closer to physical reality than our modern monetary approach, and has the advantage of *avoiding the "valuation problem."* For this reason it is more appropriate to regard such a token aggregate as a "superaccount," not unlike a balance sheet—it may be no coincidence that we still speak of the "content" of an account as well as the "content" of a balance sheet.[8] Of special importance is the fact that those "aggregates" had a *dual* meaning— something that may not have escaped the Sumerians: in its details, it revealed individual assets, in its totality it revealed an equity or part of it.

The entity behind such an equity was either a city or temple government or a personal or family unit.[9] The levying and paying of taxes was possibly based on the farming out of temple assets to individuals (the punishment by beating in the case of refusal or inability to fulfill one's repayment or tax obligation is documented in ancient pictures). But since these "superaccounts" would not have reflected the *total* equity of a temple, further aggregation of all those envelopes and string systems within a single precinct would have been

---

extraordinarily wide range of markings which they bear" [Schmandt-Besserat, 1986, p. 34].

[7]Etsuzo Kishi, in discussing the Renaissance "prototype of the double-entry method"—mainly by V. Mennher [1550]—emphasizes that under this method "[c]ash, credit and debit are to be managed separately from goods. This is derived from the tradition of the ancient Roman empire" [Kishi, 1984, p. 353].

[8]A reviewer of this paper referred in this connection to Roger North's *Gentleman Accomptant* [London, 1714] which states that: "Cash is from the Italian Cassa or Chest, in which they keep their Specie of Money; and it is a pleasant Metonymy, when Chest is full of Money." Here too the linguistic root of an accounting term lies in a physical object with a potential "content."

[9]"The evidence also indicates that plain and complex tokens were managed by different sets of hands within the Sumerian temple administration, the plain tokens belonging to the pens and granaries whereas the complex sort pertained to the workshops. Indeed complex tokens clearly seem to be associated with the world's first system of coercive taxation and redistribution of goods" [Schmandt-Besserat, 1986, p. 34].

necessary. The IOU nature of such token aggregates and of the subsequent clay tablets is also documented [cf. Schmandt-Besserat, 1986, p. 34]. From younger archeological records, one may infer the possibility that the tokens or token aggregates were handed over as receipts to the debtor and voided once the debt was *fully* "paid" (just as it was the case with the later clay tablets. (See footnote 16.)

THE LOGICAL FORM OF ECONOMIC AND ACCOUNTING TRANSACTIONS

These recent archeological discoveries certainly have put accounting into the focus of the earliest history of counting, writing and civilization. But, beyond this, they have major significance for understanding the origin and the very foundation of the input-output structure of modern accounting.

Since the late fifties I have endeavored to demonstrate that *the foundation of accounting is not to be found in the techniques of double entry but in the logical form of a transaction* [cf. Mattessich 1957/82, 1964/77, 1984, 1987, 1988, etc.].[10] This structure manifests itself *empirically* in such economic events as sales and purchases, investment and debt transactions, production and other transfer processes, etc. But at the same time this same structure can *conceptually* be represented not only in form of journal and double entries but also in form of matrices, algebraic equations, flow diagrams or networks, and vectors.[11] More recently, see Balzer and Mattessich [1991], we have tried *to overcome the diversity* of the considerable number of axiomatization attempts in accounting, by conforming with the tenets of "epistemic structuralism"—see, for example, Balzer, Moulines and Sneed [1987]— which successfully axiomatized the foundations of a series of other empirical sciences. This approach also distinguishes strictly between the *economic transactions* of real (physical and social) entities and its conceptual representation by means of accounting transactions.

---

[10]Recent reference to this "more abstract outlook" for the present and future computerization of accounting can be found by Leech [1986] and Mepham [1987].

[11]A set-theoretical analysis of this "flow" or "input-output" structure in terms of ownership and debt relations, etc., is found in Appendix A of Mattessich [1964/77, pp. 448-65]. To this Willett [1987, pp. 159, 162] offers the following remarks: "Mattessich's formal theory of accounting . . . predates Ijiri's and was probably the first serious attempt to axiomatize the discipline . . . [p. 159]. The two most famous and ambitious attempts to axiomatize conventional practice [Ijiri, 1965; Mattessich, 1964] have *both* been *transactions based*. They provide certain insights into the principal elements . . . . The most important contribution of Mattessich's theory was his attempt to define, albeit indirectly, the basic elements of the accounting structure in qualitative terms. *In particular a debt claim is defined* [1964, p. 449] as the value of some function—such that—$(e_i, e_j, T) = v_{ij}$, where e_i, e_j are accounting entities and T is a time interval, and v_{ij} is a value [p. 162]" (our italics).

The preceding recapitulation has shown that the logical form of a transaction has already manifested itself in prehistoric data processing systems. Since the ancient people of the Middle East exploited the *transfer of clay tokens from one location to another* to represent various economic transactions, there can be little doubt that *an input-output structure dominated those early accounting systems.* Of course, one might argue that this is trivial since the transfer of services or commodities, from one person or place to another, is already endowed with such a duality. But this objection fails to grasp the essential point: the objection refers only to empirical structures and events and misses *the crucial idea of duplicating the input-output of actual commodities through the input-output of tokens by means of which conceptual representation of this duality becomes possible.* Once this decisive fact of the input-output principle is recognized, it is a secondary problem, whether the ancient people of the Middle East possessed a double-entry system or not.[12] Nevertheless this point shall be examined in the section on the origin of double-entry record keeping. Yet before doing so, some connections between two kinds of duality must be explored.

PHYSICAL DUALITY AND SOCIAL DUALITY

Physical Reality and the First Type of Duality. The first kind of accounting duality arises out of the physical aspects of the output of a commodity from one place, and its input to another. In general, it expresses the one-to-one correspondence between a physical economic transaction as an empirical event (such as a sale and purchase, or the transfer of goods and services from one department or process to another), on one side, and some representational scheme—be it an accounting transaction of a token accounting system of Mesopotamia or a computerized matrix accounting system in twentieth-century America—on the other side.

Social Reality and the Second Type of Duality. The second kind of duality does not seem to arise out of a physical transfer, but of the fact that every asset belongs to somebody, and therefore is by its very nature simultaneously an equity or part of it. While the first type (involving the mere transfer of goods) possesses undoubtedly a manifestation in physical reality in the broadest sense, this is not the case with regard to the second type of duality arising out of activities such as owning and investing or lending and borrowing—all resulting in *social* relations. For those experts who accept social relations as real (as most accountants seem to do), this second duality also yields economic transactions that are representable by accounting transactions. Thus contrary to common belief, accounting is not based on a single

---

[12]The significance of the *input-output principle* for double-entry accounting is well recognized in the literature, e.g.: "The writer wishes to emphasize the merit that comes from understanding a double-entry bookkeeping as an input-output system of data calculating the amount of capital charged" [Kishi, 1984, p. 359].

(physical) duality but succeeded in integrating (perhaps subconsciously) *three separate dualities* two of which are "social." And there are two major justifications for accepting them as transactions:

(1) Double classification arises in accounting from three different relationships, each of which has by sheer coincidence (or, if you like, by virtue of their very nature) *two* dominating dimensions:

    (i)   the *physical transfer* of goods and services, connecting an *input* to an *output*;

    (ii) the *debt claim*, connecting a *debtor* to a *creditor*; and

    (iii) the *ownership claim*, connecting a *resource* (asset) to an *owner*.

The items (ii) and (iii) give justification for calling those social dualities transactions. Since both belong to social reality, they could be regarded as a single type of duality, but the social and legal differences between them are basic enough to avoid such a combination (e.g., the one is usually a financial-legal relation between *two persons*, while the other is a legal or quasi-legal relation between *a person and an object*.

(2) Another justification may be found in the existence of a link between physical and social transactions. Yet what is this link? Investing and lending activities usually result in the transfer of some commodity or a purchasing power through which a commodity can be acquired; and for the following two reasons the duality is no less present in those more abstract transactions: first, any borrowing is ultimately matched by some lending, and any investing by some ownership; and second, more importantly, debt and owner's equities are *internalizing* what otherwise would be an *external physical* duality (i.e., a transaction from one entity to another). This peculiar relationship can be illustrated by Exhibit 6—adapted from Mattessich [1964/77, p. 455]—which reveals both the *internal* (or *intra-entity*) as well as the *external* (or *inter-entity*) flows or transactions.

Explanation to Exhibit 6: This combined matrix represents the following inter- and intra-entity transactions of two entities E_1 and E_2 doing business with each other. The matrix shows *the credits in the rows and the debits in the columns*.[13]

(1) Investment of owner's equity by entity E_2 in entity E_1 by handing over some machinery.

(2) Entity E_1 receives raw material from E_2 on a credit basis.

(3) Entity E_1 supplies some finished goods to E_2 in cancellation of some of its debts against E_2.

---

[13]This accounting convention (in contrast to the later "Gomberg convention" which uses the rows as debits and the columns as credits) was first adopted by DeMorgan [1846] and in our century by Leontief [1951] as well as Mattessich [1957/82 and 1964/77].

Exhibit 6
Accounting Matrix of Two Entities with Inter-Entity As Well As Intra-Entity Flows

		Entity E_1					Entity E_2					
		RM	FG	Ma	R/P	OE	RM	FG	Ma	R/P	Invst.	OE
Entity E_1	Raw Materials											
	Finished Goods				(3)			○				
	Machinery											
	Rec./Payables	(2)								(×)		
	Owner's Equity			(1)							(×)	
Entity E_2	Raw Materials	○								(2)		
	Finished Goods											
	Machinery			○							(1)	
	Rec./Payables				(×)			(3)				
	Investments											
	Owner's Equity											

The rows are Cr-sides, the columns are Dr-sides.

The intra-entity transactions are recorded for each of those two entities and bear the pertinent *sequence numbers in a circle*. Since the entities are considered to be independent of each other, each event must be recorded twice—even in a two-dimensional matrix (once for E_1, the second time for E_2). But the matrix also reveals in the *empty circles* the, yet unrecorded, physical flows (of machinery, raw materials, and finished goods from one entity to another—i.e., the inter-entity transactions).

However, if the two entities were to merge and become *merely two departments of the same firm*, only those transactions (with empty circles), *instead* of the corresponding ones with numerals, would be recorded (this proves that there are *physical* flows behind the inter-entity transactions which themselves reveal only *abstract* flows, e.g., between such different "things" as Machinery and Owner's Equity). Another consequence of the assumed "merger" is that the transactions marked by a ⊗ (a second kind of what were originally inter-entity transactions), would be required *to cancel out* the claims or obligations between the two departments (formerly two separate entities).[14] To show how *inter- and intra-entity transactions are linked with each other*, we connect them (in Exhibit 6) with horizontal and vertical *dashed* lines. Hopefully this analysis has clarified those connections and shed some light on our previous assertion that the two dualities, although by no means identical, are closely tied to each other (some experts may even consider them as two aspects of a basically physical duality). Above all, it should now be obvious that the transactions involving debt or investment relations, though not themselves social events can be linked—some would even say reduced (e.g., in the case of a merger)—and traced to physical inputs and outputs—for details see Mattessich [1991a].

Whether the representation of the physical commodity transactions *preceded* historically the more abstract or, better said, social transactions, is not known. But there is evidence that by 3250 B.C.—the time when the sealed clay envelopes and string systems emerged—accounting had already incorporated ownership claims as well as stewardship or debt relations—the latter two may not have been clearly discerned at this early stage as two different legal relations. The importance and function of the *clay seals* on the envelopes as well as on the string aggregates, can be inferred from later times when a refined cuneiform writing offers detailed evidence and explanation about the legalistic or semilegalistic function of those seals.[15] It is from those later records that the more abstract and legal relations can be inferred.

---

[14]In contrast to having separate raw material inventory and machinery accounts for each department, *no separate* receivables and payables accounts are assumed to be kept for each department.

[15]"Sumerian clay tablets by the tens of thousands (literally), inscribed with their business, legal, and administrative documents crowd the collections of these same museums, giving us much information

But the fact that both the clay envelope as well as the string aggregate were usually firmly sealed—so that the transfer from one personal account to another was impeded—is evidence that our hypothesized transfer of tokens was allowed only to authorized persons. The seal will have been kept on as long as the personal account was "inactive," but could be broken as soon as one or more transactions were recorded through the exchange of tokens. Afterwards a new seal, possibly incised with different appropriate data, was made.[16] To every piece of commercial reality (a measure of grain, a ewe or ram, a jar of oil or a piece of silver) of those ancient people, there *corresponded* a specific token in their representational accounting system. It does not matter that this system itself consisted of concrete objects (like cylinders, cones, etc.) instead of abstract, written symbols; on the contrary this intermediary step reveals to us the evolution of a conceptual system—it not only demonstrates that *abstraction is a matter of degree*, but shows how more abstract representational systems evolved from less abstract ones. The crucial thing is that we are here not dealing with the actual transfer of commodities, but with their *representation for accounting purposes*.

THE HIERARCHY OF ARCHAIC ACCOUNTS

We have previously established that every "asset account" seems to have been characterized by a specific token shape. But these accounts were not limited to purely tangible assets, occasionally they included a claim to services (the tetrahedron token seems to have represented a day of labor [see Schmandt-Besserat, 1980, p. 375]). Beyond this lower echelon of accounts, one or two higher echelons have to be distinguished.

The second level of accounts is represented by the receptacles, i.e., clay envelopes as well as string aggregates. Similar to the income statement, these would undoubtedly have been accounts of a higher echelon since they usually contained tokens of different shapes and thus summarized the content of several accounts (but unlike the income statement, they did not summarize "nominal" but only "real" accounts).

The third level of accounts can be found in the accumulation of all clay envelopes and string aggregates within one temple precinct or other entity. If all those receptacles were kept in one room, then this room would, in a way, have been equivalent to our modern balance sheet (e.g., each receptacle representing an accounts receivable and the totality representing the "owner's equity").

---

about the social structure and administrative organization of the ancient Sumerians" [S.N. Kramer, 1963, p. 379].

[16]This representational method can even be associated with the *correspondence theory of truth* as promulgated by Bertrand Russell and developed in Wittgenstein's [1922] Tractatus—for further details on this relation to the correspondence theory see Mattessich [1987 and 1988].

But how about income measurement? Those archaic accounting systems do not offer any direct evidence, neither for the notion of income nor for any attempt of its measurement. However, it may well be possible that, whenever a debt relationship was entered and the pertinent token receptacle was created, a token was added by means of which the pertinent aggregate did not constitute the original debt but the final debt, i.e., augmented by an interest or income item represented by this added token—similar to later accounting practices, e.g., during the sixteenth and seventeenth centuries, when debts were invariably recorded at their discharge value. If interest was charged at all, this scenario is more likely than the alternative of establishing the interest at the time of repayment without having any agreement and record in advance.

THE ORIGIN OF DOUBLE-ENTRY RECORD KEEPING

We have seen above that those ancient people of the Middle East had record keeping systems, the basic logical structure of which was virtually identical to that of modern double entry. But did they have some kind of double-entry record keeping? As surprising as it may seem, a good case can be made that such a double-entry system (which must *not* be confused with a double-entry *bookkeeping* system) did exist over five thousand years ago.

The original clay envelopes (ca. 3250 B.C.) had a great disadvantage: once sealed, one did not know their token content unless breaking the seal—something that was supposedly permitted only at the event of settlement [cf. Schmandt-Besserat, 1980, pp. 366, 377; Rosengarten, 1960, p. 221]. But relatively soon after the emergence of the original envelopes (ca. 3200 B.C.) it was already customary to impress the softer clay surface of those envelopes with the hardened clay tokens before putting them into the receptacle and sealing the latter (see Exhibit 3).[17] This enabled one to determine at a first glance the content of the envelope while the seal and other markings may have informed about the debtor and other details. There can be little doubt that inserting a token into a receptacle was equivalent to a "debit entry" in an asset account. Yet there were two other requirements: first, to indicate, on the outside of the clay envelope, the individual items contained in it, and second, to disclose instantaneously the total equity represented by the receptacle. By a lucky stroke these two requirements could be met in a single step: impressing the hardened tokens upon the softer, unburned surface of the clay container. The resulting indentations

[17]This inconspicuous impressing of the clay tokens upon the surface of the receptacle may turn out to have been one of the greatest steps of mankind; not only was it the *precursor* of modern double-entry bookkeeping, more importantly, it was the major impetus to cuneiform writing as well as abstract counting. And it is no coincidence that one chapter in Ifrah's [1981/87] book bears the title "Was Writing Invented by Accountants?" A question which Ifrah [1981/87, pp. 151-2] answers in the affirmative by reference to Amiet [1973].

(see Exhibit 3) are mirror pictures and true counter-entries (credit entries) on the equity side of this prehistoric record-keeping system.

ACCOUNTING AND THE PRINCIPLE
OF CONSERVATION OR SYMMETRY

This paper is concerned with the early history as well as the foundation of accounting. But the latter aspect occasionally raises the question whether the *input-output principle* of accounting might fulfill a similar function as the *principles of conservation of* physics.[18] Since prehistoric accounting *directly* represented physical transfers, and did not deal with any monetary valuation, the first kind of duality (see the section on physical reality and the first type of duality) may be regarded as reflecting such conservation. Or in other words: *the transfer of a token from one location to another, conveyed that in the act of physically transferring a commodity from one person (or institution) to another, certain qualities of that commodity were preserved.*

Yet accounting is not only concerned with momentary events but also with the changes of wealth over time. Just as the conservation laws of physics and chemistry[19] are designed to give account of what happened to the input of energy and matter, momentum, spin, etc., in terms of the corresponding output, so accounting tries to give account in terms of commodity utilization.[20] Even if some commodities get consumed, lost, or dissipated during a certain transformation, *it is that "giving accounting" of the total input in terms of the total output (or*

---

[18]Cf. Mattessich [1980, p. 233; 1984, p. 408] as well as Thornton [1985, p. 137], and Swanson [1987, pp. 82, 90, 91] who even speaks of a "matter-energy flow" in accounting.

[19]Apart from the law of conservation of matter and energy, quantum theory knows conservation principles with regard to electric charge, linear momentum, spin (angular momentum), isospin, barryon charge, muon charge, strangeness, combined parity (space reflection) plus charge reflection plus time reversal, etc. For further details see Parker [1982, pp. 38, 175-6, 891-2, 1135-41, 1213-5].

[20]Physicists freely admit that their conservation or symmetry laws imply *accountability* which for example, is greatly facilitated by such notions as "work" (force times distance): "Work is a mere bookkeeping device to keep track of transfer of energy from one thing to another" [Olenick, Apostol, and Goodstein, 1985, p. 249].

Even more startling is the following statement of "physics-accounting" which leads to the postulation of *a total zero-energy in the cosmos* (see also Tryon [1973, pp. 396-7]):

> But there is also another form of energy important to cosmology, that acts in a sense, in opposition to this mass-energy. Namely gravitational potential energy . . . . One could think of this as the supply of energy needed to push the galaxies infinitely far apart; hence it is regarded as *a negative energy on the ledger books of the universe* (our italics) [Bartusian, 1986, p. 256].

vice versa) which is crucial for every principle of conservation. To many accountants and economists is seems to be a flagrant contradiction to consider something "consumed" or even "lost" as something "conserved" (cf. for example Adam Smith's *narrow* income definition from which mere "services" were excluded because they are instantly consumed). But asserting such a contradiction would be like insisting that the second law of thermodynamics (entropy law: the increase of dissipated energy in the universe) contradicts the first law of thermodynamics (conservation of energy). Yet the fact that some energy is wasted (i.e., no longer available to do work because it is dissipated as "useless" heat) does not negate the constancy of energy in this universe. Even when the accounting process is extended to valuation (in spite of the latter's *subjective* nature), it is possible to cope with this problem. One might talk about *value accountability* of inputs in terms of outputs, *provided "wasted (dissipated) value" is included under value conservation no less than "wasted (dissipated) energy" is included under energy conservation.* Again, the criterion for "conservation" is not whether the pertinent item is useful or useless, but whether it has been accounted for or not. But accountants irritated by the expression "conservation," may substitute for it the term "symmetry"—even physicists nowadays speak of *principles of symmetry* when referring to the laws of conservation.

Since the accountability of energy and *physical reality* can be cast in terms of universal principles of symmetry, the accountability of value and *social reality* by similar means, might deepen our understanding of accounting and simultaneously shed further light on *one important aspect of physics: its function as a cosmic accounting system.*[21]

REFERENCES

Amiet, P. *Bas-Reliefs imaginaire de L'Ancient Orient d'après les cachets et les sceaux-cylindres.* Paris: Hôtel de la Monnaie, 1973.
Balzer, Wolfgang, and Richard Mattessich. "The Axiomatic Structure of Basic Accounting: Towards a Structuralist Reconstruction." *Theory and Decision,* in press for 1991.
Balzer, Wolfgang, C.U. Moulines, and J.D. Sneed. *An Architecture for Science.* Dordrecht, Holland and Boston, Mass.: D. Reidel Publishing Co., 1987.
Bartusiak, Marcia. *Thursday's Universe—A Report from the Frontier on the Origin, Nature and Destiny of the Universe.* New York: Time and Omni Books, 1986.
Boas, Franz. "Fifth Report on the Northwestern Tribes of Canada." *Proceedings of the British Association for the Advancement of Science,* 1989.
Bower, Bruce. "Calculating Apes." *Science News* (May 1987), pp. 334-5.

---

[21]For other analogies between accounting and physics see Ijiri [1989], particularly pp. 84-6, and Mattessich [1991b], Section x of "Editor's Commentary."

Danzig, Tobias. *Number: The Language of Science*. 4th ed. New York: MacMillan Co., 1959.

DeMorgan, August. *Elements of Arithmetic*. 5th ed. Appendix: "On the Main Principle of Bookkeeping." London: 1846.

Flegg, Graham. *Numbers—Their History and Meaning*. New York: Schocken Books, 1983.

Ifrah, Georges. *From One to Zero*. Original French ed., Paris: 1981. English trans., London: Penguin Books, 1987.

Ijiri, Yuji. "Axioms and Structures of Conventional Accounting Management." *The Accounting Review* (January 1965), pp. 36-53.

_____. *Momentum Accounting and Triple-Entry Bookkeeping: Exploring the Dynamic Structure of Accounting Measurement*. Sarasota: AAA, 1989.

Jasim, S.A., and J. Oates. "Early Tokens and Tablets in Mesopotamia: New Information from Tell Abada and Tell Brak." *World Archeology* (February 1986), pp. 348-62.

Kishi, Etsuzo. "Prototype of Double Entry Method by V. Mennher." In: Tito Antoni, ed., *Proceedings of the Fourth International Congress of the History of Accountancy*, Pisa: ETS Editrice, 1984, pp. 349-62.

Kramer, Edna E. *The Nature and Growth of Modern Mathematics*. New York: Hawthorn Books, 1970.

Kramer, S.N. "The Early History of Cuneiform." In: Jacquetta Hawkes, ed., *The World of the Past*, New York: Alfred A. Knopf, 1963, pp. 379-80.

_____. *The Main Stream of Mathematics*. New York: Oxford University Press, 1955.

Leech, S.A. "The Theory and Development of a Matrix-Based Accounting System." *Accounting and Business Research* (Autumn 1986), pp. 327-41.

Legrain, Léon. "Empreintes de cachets élamites." *Mémoire de la mission archéologique de Perse* vol. 16 (1921), pp. 7-8.

Mattessich, Richard. "Towards a General and Axiomatic Foundation of Accountancy—With an Introduction to the Matrix Formulation of Accounting Systems." *Accounting Research* (October 1957), pp. 328-55. Reprinted in Stephen A. Zeff, ed., *The Accounting Postulate and Principles Controversy of the 1960's*, New York: Garland Publishing, Inc., 1982.

_____. *Accounting and Analytical Methods—Measurement and Projection of Income and Wealth in the Micro- and Macro-Economy*. Homewood, Ill.: Richard D. Irwin, 1964 (reprint, Houston, Tex.: Scholars Book Co., 1977).

_____. "Management Accounting: Past, Present, and Future." In: Peter Holzer, ed., *Management Accounting 1980*, Urbana-Champaign: University of Illinois, 1980, pp. 209-40.

_____, ed. *Modern Accounting Research: History, Survey, and Guide*. Vancouver, B.C.: Canadian Certified General Accountants Research Foundation, 1984/89.

_____. "Prehistoric Accounting and the Problem of Representation: An Archeological Evidence of the Middle East from 8000 B.C. to 3000 B.C." *The Accounting Historians Journal* (Fall 1987), pp. 71-91.

_____. "Wittgenstein and Archeological Evidence of Representation and Data Processing from 8000 B.C. to 3000 B.C." Presentation at the *12th International Wittgenstein Symposium*, 1987 in

Kirchberg/Wechsel, to be published in Ota Weinberger and Peter Koller, eds., *Philosophy of Law, Politics and Society*, Vienna: Hölder-Pichler-Tempsky, 1988.

_____. "Accounting and the Input-Output Principle in the Ancient and Prehistoric World." *Abacus* (Setember 1989), pp. 74-84.

_____. "Social Reality and the Measurement of Its Phenomena." *Advances in Accounting* (1991a), pp. 3-17.

_____. *Accounting Research in the 1980's and Its Future Relevance.* Supplemtary volume to the reprint edition of *Modern Accounting Research: History, Survey, and Guide.* Vancouver, B.C.: Canadian CGA Research Foundation, 1991b.

Mennher [de Kempten], Valentin. *Practique brifue pour eyfrer et tenir liures de compt touchant le principal train de marchandise.* Anvers: 1550.

Mepham, M.J. "A Conceptual Model for Database Accounting." Working paper, 1987.

North, Roger. *The Gentleman Accomptant.* London: 1714.

Olenick, R.O., T.M. Apostol, and D.L. Goodstein. *The Mechanical Universe.* New York: Cambridge University Press, 1985.

Parker, Sybil et al., eds. *McGraw-Hill Encyclopedia of Physics.* New York: McGraw-Hill, Inc., 1982.

Peterson, Ivars. "Picture This: The Sounds of Speech Lead to Novel Ways of Representing Complex Data." *Science News* (June 20, 1987), pp. 392-5.

Piaget, Jean. *Psychology and Epistemology—Towards a Theory of Knowledge.* A. Rosin, trans. Harmondsworth: Penguin Books Ltd., 1977.

Pickover, Clifford A. "Computers, Pattern, Chaos and Beauty." IBM Reesarch Report. Yorktown Heights, N.Y.: IBM Thomas J. Watson Research Center, 1987.

Rosengarten, Yvonne. *Le Cocept sumèrien de consommation dans la vie économique.* Paris: 1960.

Russell, Bertrand. *Introduction to Mathematical Philosophy.* London: George Allen and Unwin, 1919 (10th ed., 1960).

Schmandt-Besserat, Denise. "The Earliest Precursor of Writing." *Scientific American* (1978), pp. 50-8.

_____. "The Envelopes that Bear the First Writing." *Technology and Culture* (1980), pp. 357-85.

_____. "Tablets and Tokens: A Re-examination of the So-called 'Numerical Tablets'." *Visible Language* (1981), pp. 321-44.

_____. "Decipherment of the Earliest Tablets." *Science* (1981a), pp. 283-5.

_____. "Tokens and Counting." *Biblical Archeologist* (Spring 1983), pp. 117-20.

_____. "The Emergence of Recording." *American Anthropologist.* (1984), pp. 871-8.

_____. "Before Numerals." *Visible Language* (1984), pp. 48-59.

_____. "The Origins of Writing—An Archeologist's Perspective." *Written Communication* (January 1986), pp. 31-45.

_____. "The Precursor to. Numerals and Writing." *Archeology* (November/December 1986a), pp. 32-8.

_____. "An Archaic Recording System and the Origin of Writing." *Syro-Mesopotamian Studies* (1977), pp. 1-32.

Smith, David E. *History of Mathematics*. vol. 1. Boston, Mass.: Ginn &
    Co., 1951.
Swanson, G.A. "Accounting Information Can Be Used for Scientific
    Investigation." *Behavioural Science* (1987), pp. 81-91.
Thornton, D.B. "R.V. Mattessich, Modern Accounting Research: History,
    Survey and Guide." *Contemporary Accounting Research* (Fall 1985),
    pp. 124-42.
Tryon, Edward P. "Is the Universe a Vacuum Fluctuation?" *Nature*
    (December 1973), pp. 396-7.
Vallat, F. "The Most Ancient Script of Iran: The Current Situation."
    World Archeology (February 1986), pp. 335-47.
Willett, R.J. "An Axiomatic Theory of Accounting Measurement."
    Accounting and Business Research (Spring 1987), pp. 155-71.

APPENDIX A

Chronological Table:
Evolution of Accounting and Symbolic
Representation in the Middle East

I   8000 B.C.: *Simple clay tokens of various* shapes (spheres, disks,
     cylinders, triangles, rectangles, cones, ovoids, and tetrahedrons,
     each standing for a unit of a specific commodity), accounting for the
     stocks and flows of agricultural goods and services—coinciding with
     agricultural revolution.

II   3300 B.C.: *Complex tokens with incised lines or punctations* (and
     occasionally perforated) appear in the old as well as some *new
     shapes* (parabolas, vessel forms, trussed duck forms, bent coils,
     etc.)—coinciding with first monumental architecture and the *rise of
     temple governments*, indicating a need for greater accounting
     accuracy.

III 3250 B.C.: *Emergence of sealed aggregation devices: Hollow clay
     envelopes* (bullae) to safeguard accounting tokens (usually
     representing *agricultural products* that were common "currencies")
     and *sealed string systems* for safeguarding perforated accounting
     tokens (usually representing *manufactured goods* and *labor units*).
     Both devices were impressed with personal or institutional seals and
     often used simultaneously *to give evidence for inventories and debt
     claims as well as the equities behind them*—indicating increasing
     legalism and bureaucratism.

IV   3200 B.C.: *Surfaces of clay envelopes are also impressed with each
     token to be enclosed* (or each token shape combined with a number
     symbol) to reveal from outside the assets and equity represented by
     the token content—constituting a kind of double-entry system
     (actual tokens inside represent assets, negative tokens impressed
     outside represent counter-entry of pertinent equity), as well as the
     beginning of *abstract* counting and writing.

V   3100-3000 B.C.: First pictographs incised in soft stones (very rare
     in contrast to the abundance of clay tokens and early pictographs in

68

clay). *Emergence of archaic cuneiform writing*, using many symbols identical or similar to negative token impressions. Continuing use of both token accounting systems.

NOTE

Illustrations of clay tokens and token accounting systems from Susa, Iran ca. 3350–3200 B.C., courtesy Musée du Louvre, Department des Antiques, were kindly put at the author's disposal by Professor Denise Schmandt-Besserat, University of Texas at Austin.

CHAPTER 4

Archeology of Accounting and Schmandt-Besserat's Contribution

Archaeology of accounting and Schmandt-Besserat's contribution[1]

Richard Mattessich

Abstract

The publication of Denise Schmandt-Besserat's book *Before Writing* (1992, vols I and II) is the occasion for first reviewing her archaeological work (see Part I), and then interpreting and commenting on it from an accountant's point of view, emphasizing further evidence that a kind of double entry recording existed 5,000 years ago (see Part II).

Schmandt-Besserat recognized that 'tokens' (small clay counters) constitute an accounting system, widely used in the Near East from about 8,000 BC to 3,000 BC, that existed for five millennia. She also drew parallels between the shapes of the tokens and those of the first signs of writing, establishing accounting as the prerequisite and impetus to writing and abstract counting.

A third part offers (in addition to the notes for Parts I and II) a summary of the 'Stages in the Evolution of Accounting and Symbolic Representation in the Prehistoric Middle East' (Appendix A) and of 'Major Steps and Publications Toward an Archaeology of Accounting' (Appendix B), as well as 'Major publications by Denise Schmandt-Besserat' and 'Other references'.

PART I

Introduction

Archaeology is the scientific study of material remains of human cultures to derive knowledge about prehistoric times,[2] though occasionally the term is used in an extended, perhaps metaphorical, sense. Foucault (1972), for example, speaks of 'the archaeology of knowledge'; and Hopwood (1987), following this example, refers to 'the archaeology of accounting systems'

Accounting Business and Financial History, Volume 4, Number 1, 1994
© Routledge 1994 0958–5206

when discussing *different layers* of accounting thought and practice during the past century or so; while Power (1992: 37) uses the term 'prehistory' also in a metaphorical way.

Here, however, 'archaeology' and 'prehistory' are not used in this extended fashion, but in the sense of *digging out* as well as interpreting prehistoric and ancient objects in the literal sense. But is it meaningful to speak of an 'archaeology of accounting' in the genuine, 'prehistoric' sense; is there such a kind of archaeology? The word 'prehistoric' commonly refers to 'the time before the invention of writing',[3] and this paper shows that an archaeology of accounting, in this sense, does exist – though it is in its infancy. A major pioneer of this sub-area is Professor Denise Schmandt-Besserat (of the University of Texas at Austin); but her achievement touches many disciplines and is by no means confined to accounting. As an archaeologist (originally specializing in prehistoric clay objects) she hardly started out with the intention to contribute to accounting.[4]

Clay is such a versatile material that even man himself is claimed to consist of it. This may be religion or mythology, but the fact that accounting has its origin in clay has a more scientific basis. The reader might readily think of the thousands of tablets from ancient Sumer and Babylon, bearing early accounting records in form of cuneiform writing. Yet here I am not so much referring to those tablets – which belong to history rather than prehistory – as I am talking about their precursors: clay tokens (small objects) of diverse shapes and hollow clay 'envelopes' containing those tokens, sealed strings with perforated tokens, as well as tablets *impressed* with tokens.

From an accountant's point of view the surprising achievement of Schmandt-Besserat is the insight that record keeping for commodities (including labour and metals) and related accountability purposes *preceded writing as well as abstract counting*. But even more startling is her claim that *this kind of accounting was the precondition and impetus to the invention of writing as well as abstract counting*. This would make prehistoric accounting a foundation stone of culture. Such news is a potential booster to accounting – indeed, it is of such enormous magnitude that it may take time before its consequences are realized. To appreciate the archaeology of accounting fully, as well as the contribution of Schmandt-Besserat, we have to probe deeper.

Accounting before writing?

The emergence of agriculture in the neolithic age (emergence of agriculture and domestic animals), and later the foundation of early cities in the Fertile Crescent (from ancient Persia and Mesopotamia to the border of Egypt), necessitated a quantitative system of recording various commodities. The existence of those commodities in a certain location, their transfer, their ownership, as well as possible debt or ownership claims connected to such commodities or their transfer, all this had to be identified and recorded by prehistoric people. But this was a time when neither counting (in the abstract sense) nor writing existed. Which form could such an early accountability system have then possibly taken? The answer to this lies less in a detective story than in the ingenious stroke of a most astute observer. The reason why I hesitate to regard it a detective story is this: Schmandt-Besserat was originally not searching for but rather stumbled on *the origin of accounting*. Its discovery came as a fortuitous afterthought.

Mysterious clay tokens and the origin of writing

The focus of Schmandt-Besserat's research, as well as her book, is primarily the origin of writing and abstract counting; only secondarily is it that of accounting. The introduction to her book presents various myths advanced since ancient times, and designed to explain the origin of writing, generally regarded as a kind of instantaneous invention (be it by either gods or mortals). Although this notion of a relatively sudden event was kept alive until recently, William Warburton (1738) introduced, already in the eighteenth century, the first *evolutionary theory* of writing. It was a *pictographic theory* of three stages: rude picture writing as in Aztec codices, pictures representing more abstract ideas as in Egyptian hieroglyphs and refined hieroglyphs as in Chinese characters. This pictographic theory 'remained virtually unchallenged for over two hundred years' (Schmandt-Besserat, 1992: 4). Although not accepted universally, the theory seems to have survived as the dominant doctrine until 1929 when the excavations of Uruk (the biblical Erech) unearthed many cuneiform tablets as well as older tablets impressed by geometric and other forms. If the latter signs can be called 'pictures', they are those of tokens, and thus are very different from the pictures of goods and other things associated with Warburton's theory. Most of those token-pictures are *abstract* and require a separate code or convention for interpretation.

Meanwhile archaeologists working in the Near East found on many sites *small clay artefacts* (hitherto unexplained and of various shapes). Schmandt-Besserat now calls them 'tokens' (or, occasionally, 'counters'), and has illustrated them abundantly in her book. Whether in Israel, Syria, Iraq, Turkey or Iran, those artefacts were present all over the Near East in layers dating from 8,000 to 3,000 BC and even later. This ubiquity and wide dispersion obviously pointed to either the religious-cultural or the economic importance of those tokens.

Apart from individual clay tokens, which were often loosely distributed in prehistoric sites, archaeologists discovered hollow clay balls containing such tokens. The oldest of these receptacles (called 'envelopes' by Schmandt-Besserat) go back to about 3,250 BC. They all bear seals impressed on the surface – a widespread custom of the Sumerians for identifying debtors or other persons. From about 3,200 BC onwards the container surface not only bears one seal or more but, in addition, is imprinted with every token contained in the envelope.

In visiting many museums as well as archaeological sites, Schmandt-Besserat puzzled over those tokens and containers. She soon distinguished between two major types (and many sub-types) of tokens: (1) the so-called *plain tokens* (spheres, discs, cylinders, triangles, rectangles, cones, ovoids and tetrahedrons) which can be traced as far as 8,000 BC (used mainly in the countryside) and (2) the later *complex tokens* (variously incised or punctated and often perforated, also of a greater variety of forms). *Added* shapes: vessel forms, parabolas, bent coils, etc., used mainly in cities and temple precincts. These small, ubiquitous objects (c. 1 to 4 cm. in size) were carefully hand moulded of clay and hardened by burning at a relatively low temperature. At some sites only small numbers of these tokens were preserved, but at other sites (e.g. at Jarmo, Iraq, dated 6,500 BC) some 1,500 specimens were unearthed. Yet what was their precise function? Although most archaeologists working in the Fertile Crescent encountered those tokens, none had a satisfactory explanation of their former use; some deemed them to be amulets or even game figures, others compared them to suppositories.

However, a crucial paper by Oppenheim (1959) discusses a curious, oblong, hollow clay ball (called in the quote from Schmandt-Besserat below a 'hollow tablet' because its outer surface bore *cuneiform* writing). But this belonged to the *second millennium* BC and not to the prehistoric period; it was found in the late 1920s in Nuzi (north of Babylon) and contained forty-nine tokens. Strangely enough, it was accompanied by a regular cuneiform tablet[5] 'bearing the account of the same transaction, in the family archive of the sheep owner Puhisenni, son of Mapu'. This tablet listed seven different kinds of sheep and goats (21 ewes that lamb, 6 female lambs, 8 rams, 4 male lambs, 6 she-goats that kid, 1 he-goat, 3 female kids); it bore the seal of Ziqarru, the shepherd who seems to have received those small cattle from the owner.

When opening the hollow tablet, the excavators found it to hold forty-nine counters which, as stipulated in the text, corresponded to the number of animals listed.[6] This hollow tablet constitutes the Rosetta stone of the token system. The counters (Akkadian *abnu*, pl. *abnati*, translated 'stone' by Oppenheim), the list of animals, and the explanatory cuneiform text leave no possible doubt that at Nuzi counters were used for bookkeeping. Although no other example of a cuneiform tablet holding counters has ever been encountered at Nuzi, or for that matter in Mesopotamia or the Near East, Oppenheim made a case that *abnati* were commonly used in the bureaucracy. He suggested that each animal of a flock was represented by a stone held in an office in a container.

The tokens were transferred to various receptacles to keep track of change of shepherds or pasture, when animals were shorn and so on. He based his argument on short cuneiform notes found in archives that referred to *abnati* 'deposited,' 'transferred,' and 'removed'. (Schmandt-Besserat, 1992/I: 9).

But Schmandt-Besserat points out that in 1959 nobody knew the shapes of those stones or tokens, as the latter were meanwhile lost, and the original excavation report did not describe their shapes. Yet, what is the rationale for the duplication of the cuneiform tablet by a receptable containing tokens? A plausible explanation for this duplicate recording (offered by Schmandt-Besserat and other authors) is this: the clay container was probably destined for the shepherd (you might say, the debtor), while the tablet constituted the owner's (or creditor's) receipt. But why did they use a token-envelope when the latter was already out of fashion for about a thousand years or so? Well, illiterate folks (like the shepherds of 2,000 BC) could easily grasp token-accounting, whereas cuneiform writing might have been legible only to more sophisticated people.[7] Tokens are tangible and relatively easy to understand; and this may have been the reason for their survival as an *auxiliary* accounting device in the historic period.

Amiet (1966), the teacher of Schmandt-Besserat, made the leap from Oppenheim's second millennium stones to the counters or tokens of the fourth millennium of Susa, interpreting them as 'calculi' and representing commodities. But now the geometric shapes of the counters were revealed, and their prehistoric nature was manifest. Amiet even made the suggestion that those calculi might be an antecedent of writing.

The task to fill the gaps, and gain the insights necessary for a complete picture, fell upon Schmandt-Besserat. By connecting the loosely dispersed tokens (between about 8,000 to 3,500 BC) with the tokens in clay envelopes (c. 3,500 to 3,000 BC and beyond), she recognized that the tokens were the basis of a widely used accounting system that lasted for some 5,000 years (compared to *double entry bookkeeping* which seems to have existed for only 600 to 700 years). Above all, she correlated the shapes of many tokens with the imprinted or incised signs on early clay tablets. She thereby offered a kind of token dictionary (cf. Figure 1) which has perhaps even more the character of a Rosetta Stone for prehistoric accounting than the paper by Oppenheim (1959), the key significance of which remains, of course, undisputed – at least in so far as *it correlated known symbols with unknown ones.*

Schmandt-Besserat's insight to juxtapose the imprinted (or later incised) images of early historic times (the meaning of which was by this time already known) to the token shapes, the meaning of which was then still unknown to archaeologists was the crucial step. For example: the sign of a 'circled cross' incised on tablets was revealed to correspond to the token of a 'disk with incised cross'. And those relatively primitive two-dimensional

Figure 1 Tokens and pictographs

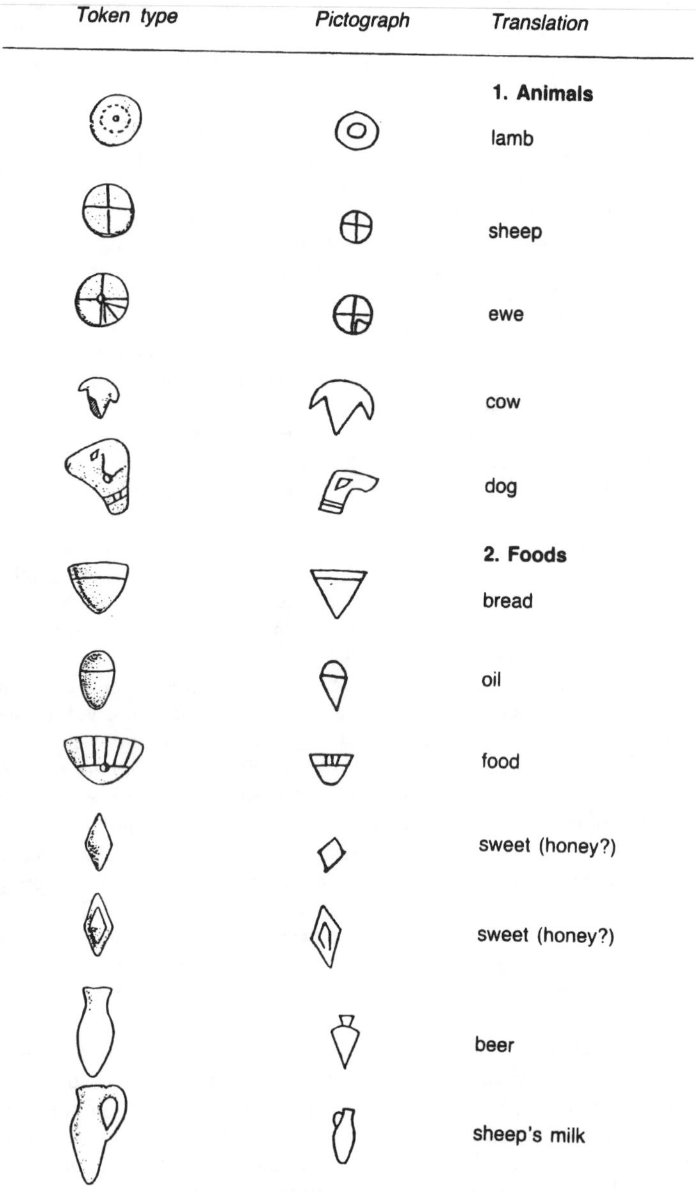

Token type	Pictograph	Translation
		1. Animals
		lamb
		sheep
		ewe
		cow
		dog
		2. Foods
		bread
		oil
		food
		sweet (honey?)
		sweet (honey?)
		beer
		sheep's milk

3. Textiles

		textile
		wool
		type of garment or cloth
		type of garment or cloth
		type of garment or cloth
		type of garment or cloth
		type of garment or cloth
		type of garment or cloth
		Wool, fleece
		rope
		type of mat or rug
		type of garment or cloth
		type of garment or cloth
		type of garment or cloth

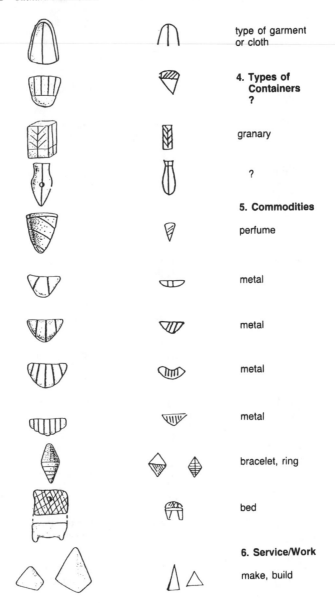

		type of garment or cloth
		4. Types of Containers ?
		granary
		?
		5. Commodities
		perfume
		metal
		metal
		metal
		metal
		bracelet, ring
		bed
		6. Service/Work
		make, build

Source Adapted from Schmandt-Besserat (1992/I: 143–8), with permission of University of Texas Press ©.

signs could directly be linked to cuneiform writings. For example, the crossed disk, or alternatively the encircled cross, stands for 'sheep'; similarly, an ovoid with circular incision stands for a 'jar of oil'; a disc with four parallel lines for wool; and so on. Meanwhile, many more shapes have been interpreted.

Schmandt-Besserat showed that token accounting was the forerunner and impetus to writing as well as counting in the abstract sense. Finally, she collected (in almost two decades of meticulous work) an overwhelming amount of archaeological evidence to support her hypothesis. Although she produced many pertinent papers (see her bibliography in Part III of this paper), the two volumes under review are the summary of her achievements.

The advent of abstract counting

The notion that *counting* evolved in several phases seemed to have been more readily accepted than have the different stages in the evolution of writing. Schmandt-Besserat (1992/I: 184–7) characterizes three evolutionary phases of counting: (1) one-to-one correspondence (mainly through tallies, pebbles, etc.), (2) concrete counting (mainly with tokens) and (3) abstract counting (with numerals).

Counting by one-to-one correspondence

This involves the one-to-one matching between a sign (e.g. a notch on a bone, a pebble, a sea shell) and a commodity, like a goat, a measure of grain or a coconut, repeating the sign for every additional unit of this commodity. Animal bones and antlers marked with notches excavated at Palaeolithic and Mesolithic sites fall into this category.[8] This one-to-one correspondence seems to be one of the two universal principles of primitive counting (observable even in pre-school children); the other universal principle arises from the fact that many primitive tribes distinguish only between *one*, *two* and *many* when counting, thus having only a three-number notion. Schmandt-Besserat (1992/I: 185) mentions the Weddas of Ceylon (Sri Lanka), who applied this method until the past century or so. In counting coconuts, for example, they piled up a heap of small sticks, adding one stick for every coconut counted. The total of coconuts then corresponded to the total of sticks.

Concrete counting

This concerns the enumeration through concrete tokens (or even body parts and similar objects) and specific number words. Vestiges of the latter are found in many languages where *different things are counted by different sets of number words*. A striking example is Japanese but, as Schmandt-Besserat points out, even in English one still uses such expressions as 'a couple', 'a brace', 'a pair', all indicating the number two but not necessarily interchangeably (one cannot speak of 'a brace of shoes' but one can say 'a brace of pheasants'). It is noteworthy that those enumerations do not go very far, usually end with a word for 'many' (e.g. triangle, square . . . polygon) and are not used for counting but merely for classifying numerically. Hence the main characteristic of concrete counting is the identification of a set of words or tokens with a set of specific things.

Schmandt-Besserat (1992/I) believes that the notion of *cardinality* was introduced already at this stage of concrete counting:

> The hypothesis that from the beginning of the token system groups of counters were no longer the mere representation of one unit ('and one more') but expressed a cardinal number is based on my argument that certain tokens stood for sets ($x = n$). I posit, for example, that tetrahedrons, which occur in two distinct subtypes 'small' and 'large' . . . represented two different units of the same commodity. (p. 189)

Abstract counting

Only this method liberates the number symbol from a specific set of things, creating *numerals* general enough for counting anything and creating the abstract notions of 'oneness', 'twoness', 'threeness', etc. Schmandt-Besserat suggests that, in contrast to concrete counting (which may have limited counting to a score of objects or so), abstract counting knows no limits and is the beginning of arithmetic and higher mathematics. For lay persons – so familiar with our abstract numerical system – it is occasionally difficult to understand the difference between the various phases of counting; but, as Bertrand Russell mentioned, it 'required many ages to discover that a brace of pheasants and a couple of days were both instances of the number 2' (Russell 1919/60: 3). And Schmandt-Besserat (1992/I) points out that:

> [t]he accountants of Uruk IVa can be credited with creating numerals and by doing so revolutionizing accounting and data manipulation. In fact, the Uruk IVa accountants devised two types of signs: *numerals* (symbols encoding abstract numbers) and *pictographs* (expressing commodities). Each type of sign was traced in a different technique – pictographs were *incised*, whereas numerals were *impressed*, clearly standing out from the text. (p. 192)

> In fact, the impressed signs that came to represent numerals never lost their primary meaning. Instead, according to the context, they had either an abstract or a concrete value. For example a wedge preceding a pictograph was read '1' . . . but alone it stood for a measure of grain. This

proved confusing to Sumerian accountants who eventually eliminated the ambiguity by introducing a pictograph in the shape of an ear or grain. (p. 193)

Schmandt-Besserat's magnum opus

The two volumes by Denise Schmandt-Besserat (1992), *Before Writing* (vol. I, *From Counting to Cuneiform*, with 175 photos, 6 tables and 16 charts, xv + 269 pages, price $ 60, and vol. II, *A Catalogue of Near Eastern Tokens*, xxxvi + 416 pages, with 16 photos illustrating 527 tokens, price $ 85, both 8.5″ by 11″), constitute the first comprehensive and systematic study of clay tokens (and pertaining envelopes). It is based on the examination of 116 sites in the Near East and the analysis of no less than 8,000 specimens.

Volume I begins with a foreword by William W. Hallo, an Assyriologist from Yale University, and an introduction discussing various myths on the origin of writing and the pictographic theory attempting to explain it.

Part I deals with the evidence and explains the nature of various types and subtypes of tokens. A detailed account of the evolution, manufacture and distribution of the tokens as well as token collections is offered. The distinction between plain tokens and complex tokens is carefully analysed, and the types of settlements (where tokens and related artefacts were found) are discussed in detail. The clay envelopes, harbouring those tokens, and the alternative accounting system of sealed strings of tokens are discussed in a common chapter. The final chapter of this part covers the next evolutionary stage, the impressed tablets, their discovery and chronology as well as many other details such as the meaning of signs (cf. Figure 1).

Part II offers the interpretation (but not from an accountant's point of view). It discusses the evolution of symbols and signs from various layers of prehistory and is seen as no less than the revolution attained by new ways of recording and storing information. Another chapter gives insight into the socio-economic implications of token accounting (cf. Schmandt-Besserat, 1992b). A further chapter deals with the problem of counting and the emergence of writing. It emphasizes the linguistic and anthropological as well as philological evidence. The final chapter of this part summarizes its subject matter by examining the role of tokens in prehistory and their contribution to archaeology.

Part III consists of drawings, charting 16 types and many subtypes (vol. II lists over 480 such subtypes) of tokens. It gives an overview of the different *variations* of cones, spheres (including partial spheres), discs, cylinders, tetrahedrons, ovoids, quadrangles, triangles, biconoids, paraboloids, bent coils, ovals and rhomboids, vessel forms, tool forms, animal forms and miscellaneous forms. The volume closes with end notes and an index.

Volume II offers a comprehensive catalogue of clay tokens (but *not* of other artefacts such as envelopes, etc.), mainly collected directly from museums in the United States, Canada, Europe and the Near East, occasionally complemented by site reports or other communications from excavators. The purpose of this catalogue is twofold:

(1) it supplies scientific evidence for supporting Schmandt-Besserat's hypothesis, presented in previous publications and refined, brought up-to-date and summarized in vol. I (1992);

(2) it offers, for the first time, a comprehensive token database together with a meticulous description and assessment of the token assemblage, its strength and weaknesses. The data are classified by countries; archaeological sites; token types and subtypes; descriptive features such as size, material, numbers at each site; whether perforated or found in connection with envelopes; chronology and stratigraphy; as well as the museums where those tokens are now located; and the references mentioning some of those tokens.

Schmandt-Besserat's hypothesis (for its first outline, see Schmandt-Besserat 1977, 1978, 1979) has not remained unchallenged. It was attacked by Lieberman (1980) who contested that the meanings attributed by Schmandt-Besserat to tokens are the same as those of impressed, incised and cuneiform tablets. Lieberman also believed that the idea that tokens represented commodities is mere speculation.[9] Further reservations were advanced by Gelb (1980), Brandes (1980), Schendge (1983) and others. But Professor Hallo (1992) points out in the foreword that Schmandt-Besserat in her continuing research and gradual refinements 'confronted all of these challenges. She has identified envelopes, notably from Susa and Habuba Kabira, impressed with non-numerical tokens, indeed with the very tokens enclosed inside' (p. x). Hallo also adds that

> [n]ot trained as an Assyriologist in her own right, she [Schmandt-Besserat] has wisely sought the collaboration of specialists in cuneiform writing and the Sumerian language, including Margaret Green, a former member of the Berlin team dealing with the archaic texts from Uruk. These texts may be said to stand midway between the tokens of the neolithic period and the fully evolved cuneiform script of the Early Dynastic and subsequent periods in Mesopotamia. The case for linking the tokens via the archaic Uruk texts to the clearly intelligible logograms of the third and second millennia is today substantially stronger than when the first tentative suggestions were advanced in the 1970's. In a special issue of *Visible Language*, devoted to 'aspects of cuneiform writing' in 1981, this point was already recognized by Green and Marvin Powell. Powell's defence of the theses (its *ad hominem* argument apart) is particularly important for its numerical aspects, given his long involvement with the evolution of cuneiform numeration systems in the historic period.

But what about the rest of the hypothesis? Here its latest refinement as first elaborated in the pages of this book is crucial. In effect, we are offered a credible hypothesis that provides a possible, even plausible evolutionary model, not only for the emergence of literacy but of 'numeracy.' (Hallo, 1992: x–xi)

PART II

Commodity accounts, equity accounts and double entry in prehistoric times

Before offering my own inferences from an accountant's point of view, let me first *summarize* Schmandt-Besserat's hypothesis: The clay tokens (of different shapes, with increasing variety as time progressed, and used abundantly between 8,000 and 3,000 BC) represented various commodities. Before 3,250 BC the tokens were presumably kept in perishable containers, but after this date they were preserved in clay envelopes, each representing a commodity aggregate owed by one person to another or, more often, owed to a temple precinct (as most of these envelopes were found in ancient temple sites).

However, simultaneously with the envelopes there existed an alternative system, using the same tokens but perforated, stringed and held together by a sealed blob of clay. In conformity with later and confirmed practice, the debtor was identified by the seal (wrapped around the envelope or impressed on the blob connecting the ends of the strings). Obviously, the advantage of the alternative accounting device lay in the instant visibility of the debt and the individual assets it consisted of.

By 3,200 BC the envelope (as an IOU) was also improved for the sake of quicker content identification. By this time the surface of the clay ball revealed not only the debtor but also the content. This was achieved by impressing each token on the outside of the envelope before putting it into the receptacle, enabling a quick identification of the entire debt (i.e. the equity owed) without opening, hence breaking the envelope.

As the shapes of various kinds of tokens were fairly well standardized all over the Fertile Crescent, I established (in Mattessich, 1987/90: 77/ 252)[10] that each *shape* had then the same function nowadays fulfilled by the commodity *account* of a specific type. As I am not sure whether this point has been clearly enough presented or fully grasped, I take this opportunity to elaborate it further. Although Schmandt-Besserat refers on several occasions to the envelopes, stringed bullae and tablets as 'accounts', she never refers to the shape of the tokens as fulfilling the function of accounts.[11] Yet these shapes do represent *asset accounts in the generic sense*.[12]

While in most cases the envelopes, etc., represent debt (or ownership) equities, i.e. a *social reality*, the token shapes are commodity accounts, thus representing a *physical reality*.[13] It seems that laymen (including archaeologists) find it easier to associate an account with a debt or ownership claim than with a commodity. But pure commodity transactions (e.g. the exchange of sheep for a goat) are relatively few in internal accounting systems, compared to those involving equities (e.g. the transfer of a sheep from one shepherd to another, when each shepherd is regarded as a kind of debtor).

In a later passage (Mattessich, 1987) it was deduced that the ancient Sumerians practised a kind of *double entry* record keeping some five thousand years ago:

> This means, first of all, that *those ancient people of the Middle East had record keeping systems, the basic logical structure of which was virtually identical with that of modern double entry* (footnote omitted). One might reply that the transfer of ordinary goods, from one person to another, already possessed this logical structure which we call the *input-output or duality principle*. This is perfectly correct, but *the ingenious stroke was to transfer this idea or principle from actual commodities by a one-to-one correspondence to a conceptual system of representation*. Once this crucial fact of the *input-output* or *duality* principle has been established, the question whether the ancient Sumerians or any other tribe used (more than five thousand years ago) a *double entry system*, is of secondary importance.
>
> However, a good case can be made that even *double entry* (in the *literal sense* of the word) *emerged as early as 3200 B.C.* From this time stem the earliest clay envelopes ... that bear on their surface the impressions of the tokens contained inside. Putting those tokens into an envelope undoubtedly meant the recording of quantities of various assets, or what we today would call 'making debit entries.' But apart from this, there were two further needs: (1) to reveal from outside the hidden content of the envelope, and (2) to reveal at a glance the entire equity represented by the envelope – as far as such an aggregation is possible without a common denominator. By sheer coincidence both of these functions could be fulfilled by a single act, namely by impressing the hardened tokens into the surface of the softer clay envelope. If this interpretation is correct, then those 'mirror impressions' can be regarded as genuine counter-entries (in this case, credit entries) on the equity side of such an accounting system. (Mattessich, 1987: 80–1)

Double entry before 3,000 BC? This must appear outrageous to many accountants and lay persons alike. Of course, it was *not* 'double entry *bookkeeping*' as neither writing nor books were in existence at that time. Nevertheless, commercial transactions were rendered in a dual fashion, and I should like to reinforce my argument in the following way (also summarized in Figure 2).

1. The rich evidence so far accumulated leaves little doubt that commodity transactions were conceptually represented by the transfer of clay tokens. The paper by Oppenheim (1959), in particular, shows that tokens were used to reflect the *physical input and output of assets*. See, for example,

Figure 2 Summary of double entry features of token system

PHYSICAL REALITY (transfer of assets):

Output of tokens from envelope A: equivalent to a **Credit** in account A

Input of tokens into envelope B: equivalent to a **Debit** in account B

Token shape indicates type of **asset account** (e.g. 'sheep', 'cloth')

Number of tokens indicates how many **units** (of sheep, cloth, etc.)

SOCIAL REALITY (ownership and debt claims):

Impressing token shapes on the outside of envelope: equivalent to a **Credit** in an equity account, recording the existence of a debt or ownership relation on the asset (indicated by the token inserted – see next line).

Inserting tokens in envelope: equivalent to a **Debit** in an asset account (corresponding to token shape), connecting the physical reality of an asset with the social reality of a debt or ownership claim (see above) – just as in modern double entry bookkeeping.

CONTROL FEATURES:

Empirical control: taking of inventory (e.g. counting of assets, e.g. sheep in pasture A) and comparing with content of sheep tokens in envelope (e.g. envelope A). If the two do not perfectly correspond in numbers and shapes, an empirical discrepancy is established (i.e. either some asset item or items are missing or some token or tokens are lost or were erroneously added, etc.)

Tautological control: counting tokens in envelope A and comparing with impressions on the surface of envelope A. If the two do not perfectly correspond in number and shapes, an analytical recording error has occurred (i.e. either the scribe forgot to impress some tokens on the surface or impressed too many, or he forgot to insert a token already impressed, etc.). But if all has been entered properly, the impressions and insertions will match for the same tautological reason that gives rise to the equality of all debits and credits in the trial balance, etc., of a *monetary* double-entry accounting system.

the quote from Schmandt-Besserat (1992: 9) on page 9 above. There it was suggested that the transfer of a small cattle from one pasture to another was represented by the transfer of the pertinent token from one envelope to another.

The *conclusion* is inevitable: the *input* of, let us say, the token for a sheep into an envelope (representing, for example, a pen or a pasture A) corresponds to a credit of the 'Sheep account' – here the *shape* of the token characterizes the account in the generic sense – and the charging or debit of 'Pasture A Account'; while the eventual *output* of this token from the same envelope would mean a credit to account A, and the *input* of this token into another envelope (say, for pasture B) would be equivalent to a debit to 'Pasture B Account'.

No one can deny that this is 'double entry recording' of the transfer of *physical objects* (real small cattle) from one location to another – at least in the sense that it fulfils the requirements of all three constituents of this expression: 'double', 'entry' and 'recording'. Of course, it is *not* a 'double entry accounting system' in the modern sense, where a tautological control checks whether the *monetary* values were entered equally on both sides.[14]

But to take such a *monetary* control as the criterion for deciding whether something is a system of 'double entry recording' would not only be a grave misinterpretation of this expression, but would mean to get stuck on the surface. The *essential* characteristics of a system of 'double entry recording' (in our sense) are structural as well as empirical; they are: (i) the *simultaneous recording of the two aspects of inputs and outputs* in different places (equivalent but not necessarily identical to 'accounts') of the system; (ii) the function of accountability together with the availability of an *empirical control* (by taking inventory and comparing it with the recording) as well as a *non-monetary tautological* control (number and shapes of tokens in the *envelope* must exactly correspond to impressions on its surface – see also 'Control features' in Figure 2). These two control features are more essential than the monetary control mentioned above; and (iii) the manifestation and *interconnection of three different dualities* (that of physical transfers, relevant for this item 1; and those of owning and owing things, discussed in item 2).

2. As to the recording of *social relations*, strong evidence indicates that the clay envelopes represented debit or property claims,[15] and that (from about 3,250 BC onwards) the totality of each claim was represented through token impressions on the envelope's surface. Indeed, the *token impressions* (i) constitute a *'converse'* and more abstract image of the tokens,[16] (ii) are *no longer separable* (i.e. individually movable) from each other, in contrast to the movability of individual tokens and (iii) *reveal* at a glance the *entire claim*.

This leads to the *conclusion* that those impressions constitute *the total equity*[17] of the individual items owed by one person to another person (or the equity owned by the latter *vis à vis* the former);[18] and the input of a token (representing a sheep) into an envelope (now representing, for example, person X) is equivalent to our debiting 'Account Receivable X' and crediting the 'Sheep Account'. Again this is a *double entry* system. Yet, in contrast to item 1, it is not for transferring physical objects but for recording social relations like *debt and ownership claims*.

3. In one respect this double entry of the token system is superior to present-day double entry bookkeeping. An 'impression' on an envelope immediately reveals itself as equivalent to a 'credit entry' *of an equity account* while the output (removal) of a token from an envelope also reveals itself as a 'credit' but to a commodity or similar *asset account*. In modern accounting, however, those two types of credit entries are not so easily distinguished, as anyone can vouch who ever taught accounting to beginners. Without the benefit of an immediate distinction, as available in token accounting,

students easily get confused between those two types of credits because one constitutes an *augmentation* (of an equity) and the other a *diminution* (of a commodity).

Another 'superiority' of token accounting appears to be the absence of valuation problems that plague modern accountants. Yet token accounting only concealed this problem, it did not solve it. What seems to be a disadvantage of the modern system is more than compensated by its greater flexibility which the common denominator of *monetary* evaluation affords (bringing with it the fringe benefit of monetary control, mentioned in item 1). However, prehistoric record keeping possessed a kind of *non-monetary valuation*: complex tokens, for example, achieved greater accuracy in discriminating between various types of cloths (and presumably *values*) by different numbers of lines incised on the token-discs (cf. Figure 1).

4. These items (1 to 3) may become still more plausible when considering that the ultimate significance of double entry record keeping lies *not* so much in entering the *same thing* twice; it lies rather in the exposition of the dual nature of every commodity transaction as well as of every debt/creditor and asset/ownership relation. This hints at the fact that double entry is not merely based on the single input-output relation of a commodity transfer. Its basis is *the combination of three very different relations* that, by fortunate coincidence, all have *two* dominating aspects. But these aspects are fairly different in each relation, as revealed by the following three items (cf. Mattessich, 1991a: 39):

(i) The physical transfer of goods and services connects an *input location* to an *output location*.

(ii) A debt claim connects a *debtor* to a *creditor*.

(iii) An ownership claim connects a *resource* (asset) to an *owner*.

A careful study of the more sophisticated version of prehistoric 'token/envelope accounting' reveals that the dual use of each token (first impressing it on the surface of the clay envelope and then putting it into the latter) reflected the *different* dual aspects of the relations listed above. Thereby the actual tokens represented a *physical reality* (commodities), while the totality of all those counter-impressions (on a specific envelope) represented the equity of this debt, hence a *social reality* (for a detailed discussion of reality issues, see Mattessich, 1991b). But at that time the legalistic distinction between debt/credit relation versus ownership relation was still blurred: money did not yet exist, and the debt had to be expressed in terms of goods. Even when repayment occurred merely in *equivalent* goods, one might speak of either an ownership or a debt/credit relation in such a non-monetary economy.

5. All this does not imply that the Sumerians were conscious of every one of those considerations, nor do I claim that this was the beginning of a continuous effort leading to double entry bookkeeping. On the contrary, it was 'progress' which prevented the continuation and further development

of this double entry aspect. As Schmandt-Besserat demonstrated, the Sumerians soon discovered that the recording goal (as well as the economic and legalistic functions) could be achieved in a simpler way than by first producing tokens and hollow clay balls (which required impressing the former onto the latter, then closing and sealing the envelope, and ultimately breaking it open). Using a flat clay tablet (instead of a hollow ball) and impressing the tokens on it (or incising the tablet with a similar shape) required only a *single* entry, but was obviously more efficient.

But by 3,000 BC even greater efficiency was achieved through substituting cuneiform strokes for the token imprints on the clay tablets. Thus these early efficiency drives had a casualty, namely double entry recording. The latter fell by the wayside at the second stage of impressing tokens onto flat tablets. Here tokens were still needed, but *they lost the function of representing assets*; tokens became *mere tools for making impressions* on the tablets – only the impressions were left *to represent* real events. Without this innovation those stumbling beginnings of recording all the dual aspects of commercial transactions might have easily been further developed. Perhaps mankind could have attained double entry bookkeeping and its controlling function thousands of years earlier.

The crucial *conclusions* of items 1 and 2 involve nothing but deductions from Schmandt-Besserat's research – they are based neither on induction nor on mere interpretation. In other words, if her findings are correct, my inferences hold by necessity. And, to disagree with these findings, one would have to refute Schmandt-Besserat's (1992) overwhelming evidence by even stronger counter-evidence.[19]

To offer an overview of both (i) the various stages in the evolution of token accounting from 8,000 BC to 3,000 BC and (ii) the major steps in 'the archaeology of accounting', I have added Appendices A and B respectively. These are followed by a *separate* bibliography of Schmandt-Besserat's major publications in this area as well as a list of *general* references.

PART III

Notes

1 I should like to express my gratitude to the Social Science and Humanities Research Council of Canada for financial support. I am also most grateful to Professor Denise Schmandt-Besserat for her advice and continued interest in my interpretation of her work.
2 Cf. *The Concise Columbia Encyclopedia* (1983: 40).
3 The term 'prehistoric' is perhaps not a particularly fortunate choice since it too has a temporal, hence historic, dimension. Indeed, were this not so, the present article would hardly appear in an historical journal.
4 Schmandt-Besserat (1922/I) discusses many aspects of her discovery as well as its implications for linguistics and communication, mathematics, anthropology,

sociology and economics. Strangely enough, she mentions neither the implications for modern accounting nor for philosophy. My own interpretations and deductions concern mainly those for accounting (cf. Mattessich, 1987/90, 1989, 1991a, 1991c) but to some extent also the philosophic *problems of conceptual representation*, of which token-accounting was one of the first manifestations (cf. Mattessich 1987/90, 1988).

5   In contrast to the genuine double entry features of token accounting (discussed in the last section), I would *not* regard this duplication as a double entry within a specific entity.

6   Starr (1939: 316).

7   See Schmandt-Besserat (1992, vol. I, note 55: 235), citing Starr (1939): 'it is likely that the tablet was meant for Puhisenni's archive and the envelope was intended for Ziqarru, who was probably illiterate.'

8   One of the earliest palaeolithic evidences is the famous 'wolf bone', c. 18 cm. long, containing 55 notches, and found in Moravia in 1937 by Karl Absalom. This is 'clear evidence that the tallying principle for numbers goes back at least thirty thousand years' (Flegg, 1983: 42).

9   Schmandt-Besserat (1992/I) proves Lieberman (1980), who is not an archaeologist, factually wrong. Because Schmandt-Besserat's volume fully documents that plain and complex tokens are both enclosed in envelopes and are therefore part of the same system of accounting. Pictographs follow tokens by 200 years; they do not precede them.

10   In the accounting literature the first mentioning of Schmandt-Besserat's early archaeological research on clay tokens seems to have been by Most (1977, 1982/86) – e.g. endnote 1 of Most (1982: 52) refers to Schmandt-Besserat (1978, 1979). Then Walgenbach, Dittrich and Hanson (1980: 6) reprinted in their textbook a page from the 1 August 1977 issue of *TIME* magazine dealing with Schmandt-Besserat's research. Next Swanson (1984) published a short paper drawing accounting historians' attention to her research. But its first interpretations and consequences from an accountant's point of view seem to have been those of Mattessich (1987, 1989).

11   The passage of Schmandt-Besserat (1992) which comes closest to hinting at (but not mentioning) 'commodity accounts' is the following: 'Accounting on the other hand involves keeping track of entries and withdrawals of commodities' (p. 170).

12   The term 'account' can be used in the *generic sense* when we speak, for example, of cash accounts in general, or it can be used in the *specific sense* when referring to the cash account of a particular firm or other entity.

13   The exception is the case (also mentioned by Schmandt-Besserat, 1992: 9) in which the envelope, bulla or tablet does not represent a person but a location like a specific pasture, shed or stable. In such cases the envelopes, etc., could be taken to represent a physical reality, unless the primary purpose is to record a debt claim towards the person responsible for the assets at this location. But it is questionable whether, at this time, the legal difference between a debt and the obligation to return *custodial* goods was clearly conceived (cf. last section).

14   However, the basic idea of such a *tautological control*, though in the non-monetary sense, *is maintained even in a double entry token system* when recording property or debt claims. This is best demonstrated by imagining an ancient scribe who ultimately checks whether *all* the tokens put into a clay envelope were actually impressed on its outer surface. Finding a discrepancy, he knows an error has occurred.

15   Schmandt-Besserat (1992) confirms this in several places (e.g. pp. 8, 108, 109) by speaking of 'accounts' in connection with clay envelopes, stringed bullae or tablets.

16   Schmandt-Besserat (1992: 191) admits that '[w]hen tokens were replaced by their images impressed on the surface of an envelope or tablet, the resulting signs were already more "abstract" than the previous clay counters.'

17   As to the claim (made by one of the reviewers of this paper) that 'the concept of "equity" can be traced to at the earliest, the fourteenth century', I have to disagree. Kohler's dictionary (Cooper and Ijiri, 1952: 196) defines 'Equity', first of all, as 'Any right or claim to assets'. That means an equity is either a property right or a debt claim, and nobody can deny that by 3200 BC or so, and even a long time before, people and institutions (e.g. temples and governments) held property rights as well as debt claims against other persons or institutions.

18   This corresponds to Mattessich (1987: 81), i.e. taking a token impression on an envelope to be a *credit* to an equity account, and the input of the token (into the same envelope) as the corresponding *debit* to an asset account. This, obviously, is seen *from the viewpoint of the debtor*, despite the fact that in most cases the owner (creditor) stored the envelope as a kind of receipt. But occasionally it was the other way around, as the case quoted from Schmandt-Besserat (1992: 9) shows – see page 9 above. There the accompanying cuneiform tablet (instead of the original envelope) was the 'owner's receipt'.

19   Professor Schmandt-Besserat, after having read this last section, confirmed in a letter (of 30 January 1993) my assertion with the following words:

> Your discussion of double-entry is now very clear to me. I think you are exactly right. There are in fact many clear examples among the archaic Uruk tablets. The texts of about 3000–2900 BC usually show on the obverse several separate accounts and, on the reverse, the total of entries/expenditures.

Appendix A: stages in the evolution of accounting and symbolic representation in the prehistoric Middle East

I   8,000 BC: *Plain clay tokens of various* shapes (spheres, discs, cylinders, triangles, rectangles, cones, ovoids and tetrahedrons, each standing for a unit of a specific commodity) which account for the stocks and flows of agricultural goods and services – coinciding with *agricultural revolution.*

II   4,400 BC: *complex tokens with incised lines or punctation* (and occasionally perforated) appear in the old as well as some *new shapes* (parabolas, vessel forms, trussed duck forms, bent coils, etc.) – coinciding with the first monumental architecture and the *rise of the state*, indicating a need for greater accounting accuracy.

III   3,250 BC: *Emergence of sealed aggregation devices*, such as hollow clay envelopes, to safeguard accounting tokens (usually representing *agricultural products* that were common 'currencies') and *sealed string systems* for safeguarding perforated accounting tokens (usually representing *manufactured goods* and *labour units*). Both devices were impressed with personal or institutional seals and often used simultaneously *to give evidence for inventories and debt claims as well as the equities behind them* – indicating increasing legalism and bureaucratism.

IV   3,200 BC: *Surfaces of clay envelopes are also impressed with each token to be enclosed* (or each token shape combined with a number symbol) to reveal from outside the assets and equity represented by the token content – constituting a kind of double entry system (actual tokens inside represent assets, token impressions on the surface are counter-entries representing the corresponding equity).

V   3,100–3,000 BC: First pictographs incised in soft stones (very rare in contrast to the abundance of clay tokens and early pictographs in clay). *Emergence of archaic cuneiform writing*, using many symbols identical or similar to negative token impressions. This stage is also the beginning of *abstract* counting and writing. Continuing use of both token accounting systems.

Note This appendix is an extended and improved version, adapted from Mattessich (1991a: 17). Dates are approximate ones.

Appendix B: major steps and publications towards an archaeology of accounting

Prerequisite steps

1621   Pietro della Valle (1586–1652) – and before him unnamed European travellers – rediscovers cuneiform writing on a mountain wall in Behistun (Western Iraq) and copies some signs.

1674   Jean Chardin (1643–1713) publishes complete groups of cuneiforms.

1761–1846   Various expeditions to the Middle East: Carsten Niebuhr (1733–1815) publishes in 1777 the first accurate and complete copies of the Behistun inpunctation of Darius I (in Persian, Elamite and Babylonian cuneiform). Although O.G. Tychsen (1734–1805), G.F. Grotefend (1775–1853) and R.C. Rask (1787–1832) each identify some signs, Eugéne Burnouf (1801–1852) and, independently, the renowned Henry C. Rawlinson (1810–1895) as well as Jule Oppert (1825–1905), Edward Hincks (1792–1866), F.J. Caignart de Saulcy (1807–1880) deciphered most of the signs – published by Rawlinson (1846).

1905–1960   Many expeditions, excavating and preserving tokens, envelopes, impressed and incised tablets as well as cuneiform tablets, etc., and *publishing pictures of tokens and envelopes at a time when such objects were considered insignificant*: see particularly the excavations reports and other publications by de Morgan *et al.* (1905), Starr (1939), Lacheman (1958) and the master's thesis of Vivian Broman (1957/85) including tokens from Jarmo.

First steps

1964   Falkenstein emphasizing that cuneiform writing was (originally) created for the exclusive purpose of recording economic transactions.

1959–1966   Publication of Leo Oppenheim's crucial paper (1959) on counters and a cuneiform envelope with accompanying cuneiform tablet from the *second millennium* BC, revealing this *envelope as a kind of IOU*, containing tokens. Amiet (1966), following Oppenheim's lead, *interpreting clay counters* in envelopes of the *prehistoric* period *as representing commodities.* Lambert (1966) identifying *impressed signs* on envelopes as *token impressions*.

1969–1993   Research and publications of Denise Schmandt-Besserat (see separate bibliography) in collecting and *interpreting* clay artefacts and evidence of the use of *tokens, envelopes, imprinted and incised tablets for purposes of commercial record keeping. Correlating the tokens with imprints and signs on archaic tablets.* Identifying the meaning of dispersed tokens from 8,000 BC (and later) with the meaning of tokens in envelopes of the fourth millennium, and *inferring the meaning of token shapes from cuneiform tablets.*

1987–1993   Interpretation of Schmandt-Besserat's research from the accounting point of view by Richard Mattessich (see references): *token shapes* fulfilling the function of *commodity accounts* (in the generic sense), *envelopes* as receivable/payable accounts containing not only the details (goods) of loans but also *representing separately (as imprints) the total equity* of commodities loaned, or stored in specific places or allocated to specific flocks, etc. Inferring the *double entry character* of prehistoric token accounting from both, the transfer of tokens (representing physical inputs and outputs) and the impression of tokens on the outside of envelopes (representing social relations).

Major publications by Denise Schmandt-Besserat

(1977) 'An archaic recording system and the origin of writing', *Syro-Mesopotamian Studies*, 1(2): 1–32.

(1978) 'The earliest precursor of writing', *Scientific American*, 238(6): 50–8.

(1979) 'Reckoning before writing', *Archeology*, 32(3): 23–31.

(1980) 'The envelopes that bear the first writing', *Technology and Culture*, 21(3): 357–85.

(1981a) 'Decipherment of the earliest tablets', *Science*, 211(18): 283–5.

(1981b) 'Tablets and tokens: a re-examination of the so-called "numerical tablets" ', *Visible Language*, 15(3): 321–44.

(1982) 'The emergence of recording', *American Anthropologist*, 84: 871–8.

(1983) 'Tokens and counting', *Biblical Archeologist*, 46: 117–20.

(1984) 'Before numerals', *Visible Language*, 18(1): 48–59.

(1986a) 'The origins of writing – an archeologist's perspective', *Written Communication*, 3(1): 31–45.

(1986b) 'An ancient token system: precursor to numerals and writing', *Archeology*, 39(6): 32–9.

(1986c) 'The precursor to numerals and writing', *Archeology*, Nov./Dec.: 32–8.

(1986d) 'Tokens at Susa', *Oriens Antiquus*, 25(1/2): 93–125.

(1986e) 'Tokens: fact and interpretation', *Visible Language*, 20(3): 250–73.

(1987) 'Oneness, twoness, threeness', *The Sciences*, 27(4): 44–9.

(1988a) 'Quantification and social structures, in D.R. Maines and C. Couch (eds) *Information, Communication and Social Structures*, Springfield, IL: Charles C. Thomas.

(1988b) 'Accounting in prehistory', *Proceedings of the Fifth World Congress of Accounting Historians*, 301/1–10.

(1988c) 'From accounting to writing', in B.A. Rafoth and D.L. Rubin (eds) *The Social Construction of Writing and Communication*, Norwood, NJ: Ablex Publishing Co., pp. 119–30.

(1988d) 'Tokens at Uruk', *Baghdader Mitteilungen*, 19: 1–75.

(1988e) 'Tokens as funerary offerings', *Vicino Oriente*, 7: 3–9.

(1989) 'The precursors of writing in one reckoning device', in W.M. Senner (ed.) *The Origins of Writing*, Lincoln, NE: University of Nebraska Press, pp. 27–39.

(1990a) 'Accounting in the prehistoric Middle East', *Archeomaterials*, 4(1): 15–23.

(1990b) 'Symbols in the prehistoric Middle East', in Richard L. Enos (ed.) *Oral and Written Composition: Historical Approaches*, Written Communications Annual 4, Newsbury Park: Sage Publications, pp. 16–31.

(1992a) *Before Writing*, Vol. I, *From Counting to Cuneiform*, Vol. II, *A Catalogue of Near Eastern Tokens*, Austin: University of Texas Press.

(1992b) 'Accounting at the dawn of history', *Proceedings of the 6th World Congress of Accounting Historians*, Kyoto 1992.

Other references

Amiet, Pierre (1966) 'Il y a 5000 ans les Elamites inventaient l'écriture', *Archeologia*, 12: 20–2.

Brandes, Mark A. (1980) 'Modelage et imprimerie aux débuts de l'écriture en Mésopotamie', *Akkadica*, 18: 1–30.

Broman, Vivian L. (1957/85) 'Jarmo figurines', master's thesis, Radcliffe College, Cambridge MA; republished as 'Jarmo figurines and other clay objects', in L.S. Braidwood, R.J. Braidwood *et al.* (eds) *Prehistoric Archeology along the Zagros Flancs*, Oriental Institute Publications 105, Chicago, IL: University of Chicago Press, pp. 369–423.

de Morgan *et al.* (see Morgan, J. de)

Falkenstein, A. (1964) *Keilschriftforschung und die alte Geschichte Vorderasiens*, Leiden: E.J. Brill.

Flegg, G. (1983) *Numbers – Their History and Meaning*, New York: Schocken.

Foucault, M. (1972) *The Archeology of Knowledge*, London: Tavistock.

Gelb, I.J. (1980) 'Principles of writing systems within the frame of visual communication', in P.A. Kolers, M.E. Wrolstad and H. Buoma (eds) *Processing of Visible Language*, Vol. 2, New York: Plenum Press, pp. 7–24.

Hallo, William W. (1992) 'Foreword', in D. Schmandt-Besserat, *Before Writing*, Vol. I, Austin: University of Texas Press, pp. ix–xi.

Hopwood, A.G. (1987) 'The archeology of accounting systems', *Accounting, Organizations and Society*, 12(3): 207–34.

Lacheman, Ernst R. (1958) *Excavations at Nuzi* 7, Economic and Social Documents, Harvard Semitic Series, Vol. 16, Cambridge: 88/no. 310.

Lambert, Maurice (1966) 'Pourquoi l'écriture est née en Mésopotamie', *Archeologia*, 12: 30.

Lieberman, Stephen J. (1980) 'Of clay pebbles, hollow clay balls, and writing: a Sumerian view', *The American Journal of Archeology*, 84(3): 339–58.

Mattessich, Richard (1987/90) 'Prehistoric accounting and the problem of representation: an archeological evidence of the Middle East from 8,000 B.C. to 3,000

B.C.', *The Accounting Historians Journal*, 14(2): 71–91. Reprinted in T.A. Lee (ed.) *The Closure of the Accounting Profession*, Vol. I, New York: Garland, 1990, pp. 246–66.

Mattessich, Richard (1988) 'Wittgenstein and archeological evidence of representation and data processing from 8000 B.C. to 3000 B.C.', in Ota Weinberger, P. Koller and A. Schramm (eds) *Philosophy of Law, Politics and Society*, Hölder-Pichler-Tempsky, pp. 254–63.

Mattessich, Richard (1989) 'Accounting and the input-output principle in the ancient and prehistoric world', *Abacus*, 25(2): 74–84.

Mattessich, Richard (1991a) 'Counting, accounting, and the input-output principle – recent evidence revising our view on the evolution of early record keeping', in O.F. Graves (ed.) *The Costing Heritage – Studies in Honor of S. Paul Garner*, Harrisonburg, VA: Academy of Accounting Historians, Monograph No. 6, pp. 25–49.

Mattessich, Richard (1991b) 'Social reality and the measurement of its phenomena', *Advances in Accounting*, 9: 3–17.

Mattessich, Richard (1991c) *Accounting Research in the 1980's and its Future Relevance*, Vancouver, BC: CGA Research Foundation.

Mecquenem, Roland Jacques de (1924) 'Fouilles de Suse (campagnes 1923–1924)', *Revue de l'Assyriologie et d'Archeologie Oriental*, 21(3): 106–7.

Morgan, J. de, G. Jéquier, R. de Mecquenem, B. Hassulier and D.-L. Graat von Roggen (1905) *Mémoires de la Délégation en Perse*, Vol. 7, *Recherches archéologiques, 2ème série*, Paris: Éditions Leroux.

Most, Kenneth S. (1977, 1982/86) *Accounting Theory*, 1st and 2nd eds, Columbus, Ohio: Grid Publishing.

Oppenheim, Leo A. (1959) 'On an operational device in Mesopotamian bureaucracy', *Journal of Near Eastern Studies*, 18(2): 121–8.

Power, Michael K. (1992) 'From common sense to expertise: reflections on the prehistory of audit sampling', *Accounting, Organizations and Society*, 17(1): 37–62.

Rawlinson, Sir Henry C. (1846) *Commentary on the Cuneiform Inscriptions in Babylon and Assyria*, London.

Russell, Bertrand (1919/60) *Introduction to Mathematical Philosophy*, 10th impression, London: Allen & Unwin, 10th ed., 1960.

Schendge, Malati J. (1983) 'The use of seals and the invention of writing', *Journal of the Economic and Social History of the Orient*, 26(2): 113–36.

Starr, Richard F.S. (1939) *Nuzi*, Vol. 1, Cambridge, MA: Harvard University Press, pp. 316–17.

Swanson, G.A. (1984) 'The roots of accounting', *The Accounting Historians Journal*, Fall 1984: 111–16.

Walgenbach, P.H., N.E. Dittrich and E.T. Hanson (1980) *Principles of Accounting*, 2nd ed, New York: Harcourt, Brace, Jovanovich.

Warburton, William (1738) *Divine Legation of Moses*, London.

CHAPTER 5

Recent Insights into Mesopotamian Accounting of the 3rd Millennium B.C.

Successor to Token Accounting; and Follow-Up to "Recent Insights into Mesopotamian Accounting of the 3rd Millennium B.C."

Accounting Historians Journal
Vol. 25, No. 1
June 1998

Richard Mattessich
UNIVERSITY OF BRITISH COLUMBIA

RECENT INSIGHTS INTO MESOPOTAMIAN ACCOUNTING OF THE 3RD MILLENNIUM B.C. — SUCCESSOR TO TOKEN ACCOUNTING

Abstract: This paper examines from an accounting perspective recent work by Nissen et al. [1993], here regarded as an extension of the archaeological research of Schmandt-Besserat [1977, 1992] and its analysis by Mattessich [1987, 1994]. The transition from the 4th millennium B.C. to the 3rd millennium B.C. featured the use of proto-cuneiform and cuneiform accounting techniques to replace the older token accounting. This research reinforces the previously made hypothesis [Mattessich, 1987] that the inserting of tokens into a clay container during the last phase of token accounting corresponded to debit entries, while the impressing of tokens on the surface of the container was meant to convey the credit total of an equity. Similarly, in proto-cuneiform bookkeeping, debit entries appear again on one side while the credit total appears on the reverse side, but this time on the clay tablets. Yet, the research also leads to the hypothesis that the *"closed* double-entry system" of token accounting could *not* be maintained in the archaic bookkeeping of the subsequent period where, apparently, a debit/credit scheme was used in which only some but not all entries had counter-entries. Finally, the paper illustrates important labor production aspects of archaic bookkeeping and cost accounting which are contrasted to modern budgeting and standard costing.

> "The best way to know a thing, is in the context of another discipline" L. Bernstein [1976, p. 3].

Acknowledgments: Financial support from the Social Sciences and Humanities Research Council of Canada for this paper is gratefully acknowledged. Furthermore, I want to express gratitude for permission to reproduce the passages quoted and Figures 1 to 3 from Nissen, H. J., Damerow, Peter, and Englund, R. K. (1993), *Archaic Bookkeeping — Early Writing Techniques of Economic Administration in the Ancient Near East*, Paul Larsen (translator), courtesy Chicago University Press (copyright) as publisher. My thanks extend also to Professor Denise Schmandt-Besserat for reading the original manuscript and for valuable advice on the dating of archaeological periods. Final thanks for many suggestions go to the editorial team (including two reviewers and, above all, the editor) of the *Accounting Historians Journal*.

Submitted June 1997
Revised September 1997
Accepted November 1997

Studying the early phases of accounting, we are not merely faced with the technological achievements of ancient people, but also experience their need for stewardship and control which they satisfied in relatively simple, yet ingenious ways. Schmandt-Besserat [1977, 1979, 1983, 1992] (hereafter SB) is the predominant researcher on prehistoric or "preliterate" token accounting, and Nissen et al. [1993] (NDE hereafter) can be regarded as an extension of this research for the "literate" period through 2000 B.C. This book has hardly attracted the attention of accounting historians and deserves to be examined.[1] Discussing the relation between "token accounting" and "archaic bookkeeping" may be a proper introduction. These two accounting systems, despite their fundamental differences, possess similarities that enable us to interpret archaic bookkeeping on the basis of my previous analysis of token accounting [Mattessich, 1987, 1994, 1995]. The literature on Mesopotamian accounting is fairly limited; the most prominent book, dealing in a relative comprehensive way with this subject, is probably Melis [1950, pp. 34-71, 111-284]. But the new archaeological evidence on administrative matters, subsequently accumulated, cries out for further expertise and analysis by academic accountants.

As to the differences between SB [1992] and NDE [1993], the latter was primarily concerned with proto-cuneiform and cuneiform accounting of the 3rd millennium B.C., while the former dealt with token accounting from 8000 B.C. to 3000 B.C. NDE [1993] did provide an overlapping section dealing with token accounting which, however, was only cursorily developed. Despite having cited two SB [1988, 1992] publications, it disregarded most of SB's findings about the original function of tokens. NDE [1993, p. 11] also expressed the belief that the "large quantities of clay tokens found in various simple geometric shapes such as spheres, rhombuses, discs, and tetrahedrons, may therefore each be thought of as the representations of different specific numerical values." This contradicts SB's evidence, which clearly indicates that the shape of a token stood for the type of commodity or a *combination* of commodity and quantity, as in the case of bulk goods such as grain where different tokens stood for different quantities of one and the same

---

[1]Vollmers' [1996, p. 4] article referred fleetingly to NDE [1993], but dealt with a much later period of accounting history.

commodity. Hence, tokens were not merely *counting symbols* but mainly *accounting symbols*, a point only hesitatingly acknowledged by NDE [1993].[2]

In many other respects, NDE were in agreement with SB's research. For example, these authors admitted that accounting tokens were originally kept in perishable containers, such as leather pouches, but later in less perishable clay envelopes (*bullae*). Those authors also confirmed SB's thesis that token accounting was a precursor to writing as well as counting and economic control.[3] Furthermore, they acknowledged the impressing of tokens onto the surface of the envelopes, stating that "occasionally, impressed signs on the outer surface of the hollow clay balls referred to the tokens stored inside them" [NDE, 1993, p. 12]. However, they failed to mention that this impressing was a crucially new development in the evolution of token accounting, constituting a "counter-entry" to the input of token-symbols into those clay receptacles. This ancient practice led Mattessich [1987, 1989, 1995] to regard token accounting as the first prototype of double-entry. Such an assumption is justified by the combination of a series of circumstances. First, the inserting of individually movable tokens, representing assets, into clay envelopes corresponds to a debit entry. Second, the impressing of the very same tokens on the surface of the clay envelope as an "inseparable totality" constitutes a credit entry, manifesting the corresponding equity. Third, the symmetry between the tokens on the inside and the impressions on the surface of the envelope confirms the correspondence to modern

---

[2]This reluctant admission is reflected in the following question and its answer: "Did these tokens already contain information about the type of the counted product, or did this information have to be added? The latter assumption may be supported by the evidence of a large number of scattered clay objects with incised patterns on their surface. Some of these clay objects were even formed into shapes that closely resemble later written signs. In such instances, these clay objects may be assumed to identify the counted object" [NDE, 1993, p. 12]. This ultimate admission brings those authors closer to SB's evidence.

[3]"Originally, however, the proto-cuneiform script was almost exclusively restricted to bookkeeping; it was an 'accountant's script'. . . . On one level, the archaic accounting script later developed into language-functional cuneiform, while on a second the system of accounting itself became more and more effective, eventually turning into a powerful instrument of formalized control of economic procedures, employing sign systems and document forms" [NDE, 1993, p. 30].

double-entry where most physical manifestations are recorded on the debit side while social relations appear on the credit side. Fourth, the token envelope can be regarded as a self-contained entity, summarizing the periodic accounting of a firm, just as a balance sheet does in contrast to an archaic accounting tablet which is neither a "closed" accounting system nor part of one. Fifth, a token envelope permits a *tautological control* (i.e., a precise matching of the tokens inside the envelope with the impressions on its surface), similar to the mathematical control of modern accounting where the debit total of a trial balance must match its credit total. Sixth, a token envelope is also amenable to a *physical control* (i.e., the "taking of inventory") by trying to match the tokens inside the envelope with the available commodities they were supposed to represent.

PROTO-CUNEIFORM BOOKKEEPING

NDE [1993] may not be the best source on token accounting of the preliterate period, but it is an excellent one on the "archaic bookkeeping"[4] of the late 4th and the entire 3rd millennium B.C. The authors carefully researched and documented this period with exciting material and new interpretations of great relevance to accounting history. They did not merely attend to the early development of "debit and credit" techniques, but also to early cost accounting, budgeting, and other accounting aspects. This work also offered discussions on several topics concerning the commercial history of Sumer and Akkad, such as prehistoric means of administration, the emergence of writing, the cuneiform script, archaic numerical sign systems and the development of arithmetic, the education of scribes, and the hierarchy of professions. Above all, it offered detailed information about the bookkeeping in the production and distribution of grain, beer, and animals, as well as the record keeping of real estate (fields) and labor services.

---

[4]Since cuneiform clay tablets are occasionally regarded as the "first books" [cf., Bram et al., 1979, Vol. 4, p. 80], the expression "archaic bookkeeping" of NDE [1993] seems to be acceptable. On the other hand, the term "token bookkeeping" would *not* be appropriate since clay *bullae* are not recognized as books; hence the term "token accounting," as used in SB [1992], is appropriate. As to the term "archaic accounting," it refers here (as it does in NDE, 1993, p. 35) to proto-cuneiform as well as early cuneiform bookkeeping and related accounting techniques.

NDE [1993] distinguished four different types of cuneiform tablets. First, small perforated tablets serve merely as tags. Second, somewhat larger tablets with numerical notation also fulfill merely auxiliary tasks. Third, and most importantly, there are larger tablets with characteristic divisions of columns and partitions, each of which reveals one specific informational unit related to the other units of the same tablet. The obverse side of these tablets, with data identified by NDE as debits, contains, in addition to verbal texts, various pieces of numerical information. The reverse side, referred to by NDE as the credit, contains the sum total of the numbers listed on the obverse. This category of tablets are the actual accounts of archaic bookkeeping. Finally, there are tablets similar to those just mentioned, but without the numerical total on the reverse, again apparently serving some auxiliary function.

According to NDE [1993], no less than ten different numerical systems were used to designate not only the units of a commodity but also its type. Indeed, for different goods and purposes different sets of numerical signs were used — one to count "discrete" objects and persons, another to count slaughtered animals, a third to count rations or wages, a fourth for measuring weights, a fifth for measuring surfaces, a sixth for time and calendar measurements, etc. These number systems used some 60 different symbols.

As to the "tautological control" present in token-envelope accounting, Mattessich [1994, p. 22] suggested that subsequent accounting systems, such as the archaic bookkeeping of the early or later 3rd millennium lost such control as they could no longer be regarded as *closed* double-entry accounting. This seemed to be confirmed by NDE [1993]. But there is sufficient evidence that later bookkeeping systems retained at least some aspects derived from the double-entry prototype of the preceding period. First, counter-entries are frequently enough found which, however, are no indication for the existence of a closed double-entry system; and second, those proto-cuneiform tablets (see Figure 1) bear the individual entries on the obverse, showing the debits, while the total is shown on the reverse side, indicating the corresponding overall credit entry. Most likely the accounting tablets emerged from the envelopes of token accounting as a kind of "unfolding" those clay balls. This is reinforced by this separate recording of individual assets on one side, with their sum total on the other side of the tablet. Token accounting also recorded individual assets on one side, inside the clay envelope, in the form of separate tokens, while on the other side (i.e., the outside surface), the set of inseparable token indentations revealed a sum total. At any rate, archaeologists have left no doubt that entries on the obverse of an entire category of cuneiform tablets are individual charges, while entries on the reverse constitute the corresponding total as a discharge, at least for proto-cuneiform bookkeeping. NDE [1993] supplied plenty of evidence for the similarity of this kind of record keeping to modern accounting.[5]

The resemblance of recording the *total* on the outside of the clay envelopes during the 4th millennium B.C. with the recording on the reverse of clay tablets during the 3rd millennium B.C. may be taken as reinforcing my hypothesis that impressing the tokens (i.e., making those inseparable indentations) on the outside constituted a collective credit, while inserting the individually movable tokens into the same clay envelope connoted the corresponding debit entry. However, if archaic bookkeeping maintains an analogous procedure, the latter need not be a closed double-entry system. Bookkeeping of the 3rd millennium B.C. matches only some but not all charges to some of the discharges, just as modern single-entry systems may do. Thus, it is very different from the closure of such a simple recording device as a clay envelope, which can be considered a *self-contained unit*. In contrast, a clay tablet of archaic bookkeeping is *not* self-contained and must be seen in context with other recordings. So far, there is no evidence that those other recordings provided closure. But had they done so, it would be extremely difficult to unearth all the matching cuneiform tablets, which are typically found broken and badly damaged in ancient city dumps.

---

[5]NDE [1993, pp. 30-32] wrote: "The tablets were seldom isolated information transmitters; rather, they almost without exception represent a part of running bookkeeping procedures in which pieces of information from one tablet were transposed to another. . . . Such texts document the most rudimentary level of accounting operations in early redistributive city-states, namely, the bookkeeping control of the receipts and expenditures of storage facilities and stocks belonging to the palace and temple households. . . . This summarizing entry [on the reverse] demonstrates another characteristic of the archaic tablets. In most cases, such entries can be identified as totals, with an accompanying sign summarizing an economic category. . . . We are aware that the sign . . . (NINDA) was used as a comprehensive sign for the distribution of various kinds of cereal rations. . . . "

EARLY DISTRIBUTION AND PRODUCTION
COST ACCOUNTING

The wealth of information presented by NDE [1993] goes beyond the constraints of this paper; here I merely summarize the gist of the bookkeeping aspects presented by these authors, together with some commentary and criticism from an accountant's point of view. One of the more complete systems (of 18 tablets), discussed and illustrated in NDE [1993], refers to an administrator, Kushim, responsible for the storage and production of beer. Some of these tablets charge the distribution of barley to several officials as various debits, with the summation on the reverse as a single credit for the discharge of Kushim's liability (e.g., figures 33 and 39 on pp. 37-39, here omitted).[6] Beside ideograms for quantities and for names of officials receiving goods, the tablet also contains an entry for the administrator and usually entries for the date or period(s) of transactions. The lack of an ideogram for zero, crucial for any numerical place-value system, resulted occasionally in arithmetical errors. The zero notion was to be expressed by an empty space which, alas, was sometimes forgotten or overlooked.

Another relatively simple account shows the charging of various amounts of barley to three officials on the obverse, while Kushim was credited on the reverse for the total amount distributed to those three officials (illustrated in figure 34, here reproduced in Figure 1). Each of the three sections on the obverse charges a different official with a specific amount of barley. Thus, each section could, alternatively, be regarded as a separate debit account. As the supply of grain was delivered by Kushim, he was credited with the sum total delivered to the other persons. The reverse side could, alternatively, be regarded as Kushim's account. Other accounts are more intricate and show the input of various ingredients (malt, hops, etc., on the obverse side) in the production of beer, as well as different kinds of beer as output on the reverse side.

---

[6]In this paper, the term "figure" refers to NDE [1993] or other sources, while "Figure" refers, throughout, to the present paper.

FIGURE 1

Sketch of Both Sides of a Proto-cuneiform Tablet Recording the Distribution of Barley to Four Officials (on the obverse, left) and the Discharge of the Administrator Kushim (on the reverse, right)

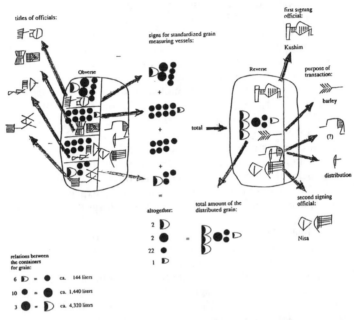

Source: Nissen et al., 1993, p. 38, Courtesy University of Chicago Press

Figure 1 contains four types of impressed numerical symbols. The smallest unit represents ca. 24 liters, the next ca. 144 liters, then ca. 1,449 liters, and finally ca. 4,320 liters. As explained in Figure 1, these numerical symbols must not be confused with the volume measures mentioned in footnote 10. Furthermore, Figure 1 reveals several incised ideograms, most of them representing names of persons or commodities. Finally, it explains the particular addition process which results in the sum total of about 14,712 liters of barley supplied by Kushim, for which he was properly discharged. Regrettably, a photograph of the proto-cuneiform tablet, on which Figure 1 is based, is not available. However, Figure 2 offers a sketch as well

as the corresponding photograph of both sides of a similar tablet, likewise from Kushim's accounts.[7]

The evolution of early accounting systems can be recognized by the marked difference between the proto-cuneiform
clay tablets (archaic texts from the Late Uruk period to the
Early Dynastic I period; i.e., 3100 B.C. to 2900 B.C.) of Figures 1
and 2; the cuneiform clay tablet (of the Early Dynastic III period; i.e., ca. 2500 B.C. to 2400 B.C.)[8], shown in Figure 3; and the
even more sophisticated cuneiform tablets (of the Ur III period,
ca. 2100 B.C. to 2000 B.C.) of NDE [1993, p. 101], here omitted,
on which the (translated) Figure 4 is based.

FIGURE 2

Sketch and Photograph of Both Sides of
a Proto-cuneiform Tablet Recording the Distribution
of Barley to the Officials Kushim and Nisa

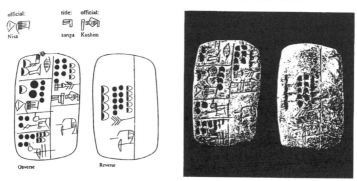

Source: Nissen et al., 1993, p. 39, Courtesy University of Chicago Press

---

[7]Kushim's signature (or sign) can be found on top of the reverse side of
Figure 1, as well as in the right uppermost field of the obverse side in Figure 2
(Does this indicate that Kushim himself received some barley?), while the
signature of the official Nisa can be seen at the bottom of the obverse and
reverse side of Figure 1, as well as in the second section of the obverse side of
Figure 2 (but apparently no signature appears on the reverse of this tablet).

[8]There may be some controversy in assigning precise dates to certain periods; according to my correspondence with SB, for example, this period should
extend from 2600 B.C. to 2334 B.C., instead of 2500 B.C. to 2400 B.C. as in NDE
[1993].

FURTHER DEVELOPMENTS AND THE USE OF
BUDGETARY PROCEDURES

The improvement of the proto-cuneiform script and the transition to cuneiform writing allowed scribes to impress and incise more details and information on clay tablets:

> Whereas during the archaic age [ca. 3000 B.C. to 2800 B.C.] the addition of further information concerning product quantities was restricted to placing a numerical sign at a predetermined place within the text format, such information was incorporated into grammatically structured sentences in later Old Sumerian texts from pre-Sargonic Lagash [i.e., before 2300 B.C.], ... [NDE, 1993, p. 47].

For the last phase of the Old Akkadian period (ca. 2250 B.C.), NDE showed tablets recording the production and distribution of various quantities of bread as well as jars of beer rationed to various individuals. What is particularly notable, from at least this period onward, is an *ex post* juxtaposition of budgeted amounts, called "theoretical" in NDE, to actual amounts produced and the recording of the discrepancy in the form of a "balancing" entry [see NDE, 1993, p. 49].

Some illustrations in NDE [1993] showed the juxtaposing of budgeted and actual data, not merely during one year but over several consecutive years, often in terms of the amounts of labor. Frequently the foremen's quotas were overdrawn, which may indicate tight budgeting with standards set at maximal performance. It also shows that the setting of standards and equivalent values, as well as the standardization of measures and budgeting procedures, had attained a surprisingly high level of sophistication. "There can be no doubt of the existence of explicitly formulated norms which were strictly adhered to. They can be reconstructed from conversions of labor performances and products into equivalent products specific to the respective sector of the economic organization" [NDE, 1993, pp. 49-51]. This is confirmed by an example from the Ur III period which shows the annual account, based on "female labor days," of a foreman supervising 36 female workers engaged in the milling of grain. The authors pointed out that the settling of a foreman's deficit was a serious matter and could result in such retribution as the confiscation of his property. The incorporation of budget standards into the regular accounting system (as illustrated in Table 1), the comparison with actual

performance, the charging of a deficit to the person responsible, and the carrying forward to future periods were typical
for state-run organizations of this time (occasionally resembling the accounting and budget procedures of 18th century
cameralism and even later). However, some of these ancient
records may remind us of modern standard costing systems,
especially those versions that combine actual material inputs
with standard (budgeted) labor inputs (see Table 1 and comments below).

THE DEVELOPMENT OF LABOR
AND PRODUCTION COSTING

Although most labor costs during the 3rd millennium B.C.
were incurred in agriculture (see next section), I shall discuss
their recording here. Those records concern the distribution of
food rations to a strictly and centrally directed labor force. NDE
pointed out that those rations were likely to be kept at a subsist-
ence level and should not necessarily be regarded as "wages"
since those workers might have been a kind of "state property."
The daily rations per person, usually one "bevelled-rim bowl" of
barley, a standard capacity of ca. 0.8 liters or more, were distributed by public granaries, through high-ranking officials, to
foremen, and finally, to the workers. Particularly noteworthy
are the following statements from NDE [1993, pp. 74-75]:

> Three . . . texts from the administrative building of
> Jemdet Nasr [around 3000 B.C.] offer a good descrip-
> tion of the way books were kept on captives employed
> in forced labor. At the same time, they provide a con-
> vincing example for the practice of setting up balance
> sheets based on individual documents. . . . This balance
> sheet again lists all the entries from both individual
> documents, totaling 27 male and female laborers. Once
> the scribe had filled the obverse side of the tablet, he
> turned it over (according to the orientation chosen in
> the figure) by making a half rotation around its vertical
> axis [a custom probably introduced for the sake of con-
> venience] and then completed another column on its
> reverse . . . . [9] After having booked the entries, the

---

[9]The use of the term "balance sheet" in NDE [1993, pp. 74-75] must be
clarified. What was meant is rather a "balancing tablet" which lists individual
workers or slaves on the obverse side of a clay tablet and their totals (apparently with subtotals) on the reverse side. From the text I discern neither any

scribe proceeded by turning the tablet upside down, recording two subtotals within the central column of the reverse. In a last step he entered the grand total of the recorded laborers in the left column of the reverse.

Again, administrative progress can be noted by comparing the "labor accounts" of the archaic period (ca. 3000 B.C. to 2800 B.C.) with those of the Early Dynastic III period (which according to NDE [1993, p. 5] seems to extend from ca. 2500 to 2400 B.C.) and, even more so, with the Ur III period (ca. 2100 B.C. to 2000 B.C.). Not only are the accounts of the latter two periods more explicit about food rationing, they also reveal the calculation process in setting standards for labor budgeting. Figure 3 shows an Old Sumerian tablet in which, again, the obverse is regarded as the debit side and the reverse as the credit side. As pointed out in a previous section, a comparison with Figure 2 reveals the change from proto-cuneiform to early cuneiform writing.

FIGURE 3

Old Sumerian Text Citing Labor Quotas in Canal Construction

Source: Nissen et al., 1993, p. 83, Courtesy University of Chicago Press

---

evaluation of the slaves in equivalent units of barley, silver, etc., nor an integration of this inventory with that of other commodities as would be done in a proper balance sheet.

Not only can such accounts be interpreted as a juxtaposition of *ex post* expectation and actual performance, it must also be regarded as the juxtaposition of production input to output, as encountered in modern cost accounting and illustrated in NDE [1993, pp. 84-85, figure 69 with translation], here reinterpreted in our Table 1. The pertinent commentary from NDE [1993, pp. 83-86] averred:

> The account is divided as usual into two distinct sections. The first section running from the beginning of the text to the fifth line of the second column . . . deals predominantly with quantities of processed raw materials, the number of employed laborers and the time they were employed. This section forms the 'debit' part of the account since raw materials as well as the labor force, expressed in (female) laborer days . . . , had to be balanced at the end of the accounting period against real delivered products and the work actually performed. In the second section of the text, the 'credits,' all finished products produced within the stated period are noted, plus the theoretical time of work necessary for their processing, the other jobs performed, all of which were totaled at the end of the section. The final step was then to calculate the difference between debits and credits. The amounts of grain and work days calculated as deficits [balance] were then recorded as such (Sumerian LÁ+NI); these probably formed the first entry of the 'debit' section . . . of the account of the following period. In some cases, such deficits had to be cleared directly, a procedure which is attested by corresponding administrative documents (the so called LÁ+NI su.ga texts = 'replaced deficit' [balance transferred]).

NDE [1993, pp. 83-85, figure 69] contained both sides of a cuneiform tablet from Umma together with a translation. But the text was presented in a highly complicated fashion, partly due to the unfamiliar arrangement of the account, and partly due to various strange measures and measure units. Some effort is required to achieve contemporary compatibility. For this reason, I have tried in Table 1 to translate this presentation into a T-account and approximate the numbers through modern measure equivalents (conversion into liters seems to be a meaningful way of explaining the clay tablet). This permits the disclosure and analysis of various discrepancies and offers an opportunity for future research.

The original translation of figure 69 into English in NDE [1993, pp. 84-85] was said to document the production accounting of a foreman, Ur-Šara, in charge of 36 female laborers processing grain, as well as doing some secondary tasks, over a period of approximately one year. The records were kept in terms of various types of cereal with conversions into barley equivalents.[10] These fixed conversion ratios may also have fulfilled a function similar to prices, especially to transfer prices

[10]This laborious footnote may be skipped by readers not interested in verifying Table 1 on the basis of Nissen [1993, figure 69 and translation, pp. 84-85]. Since this book fails to concentrate all of those data in a single place, I have summarized in the following the "conversion rates" necessary for such verification by serious students of Mesopotamian accounting.

Barley seems to have been one of the basic measures or "currency units" (others were labor hours, fish, and silver — cf., NDE, 1993, p. 51). Cereals, flour, and many other commodities were expressed in volume measures (one gur = 300 sìla; one barig = 60 sìla; one bán = 10 sìla; one sìla = approximately 1 liter in modern terms) at least for the Ur III period, while during the earlier Old Sumerian period, 1 sìla was about 1.5 liters, etc. [cf., NDE, 1993, pp. 82, 142]. As far as the conversion of "breads" into barley equivalents is concerned (see Table 1), I have relied on the following passage from NDE [1993, p. 47]: "With some reservation one would therefore translate the sentence: '40 kagu-breads baked at the rate of 50 per bán'" which would mean 1 bread is about equivalent to 0.25 sìla (or one-quarter of a liter) of dabin flour. Another passage, "3 bán of flour are needed for 90 loaves of bread" [NDE, 1993, p. 49], yields a result only slightly different, namely 0.3 sìla of dabin flour per loaf of bread.

As to the conversion of labor hours, first a distinction between female labor days and male labor days was made. This difference manifested itself, for example, in regard to "free time." Female workers got one-sixth of their total labor time off as free (cf., Table 1, lower debit side), while male workers got only one-tenth. Furthermore, the wages or rations (in barley) for labor varied greatly: "The sizes of the registered monthly rations vary between 2 bán and 2 barig (i.e., 12 bán). The great majority of the rations, however, amount to figures between 1 barig and 1 barig 2 bán, hence between 6 and 8 bán" [NDE, 1993, p. 82].

Finally, as to the conversion of finished goods into barley equivalents, NDE [1993, p. 88] provided the following conversion ratios, but I wonder whether these conversion ratios might not be contradictory. On one hand, NDE [1993, p. 88] stated, as regards various *cereals*, that "1 unit measure of dabin (flour) = 1 unit measure of še (barley)" and "1 unit of eša = 2 units of še" while, on the other hand, the book stated that "the work times required to process a unit measure of the noted grain products are . . . : for dabin 10 sìla [ca. 10 liters] per day [of female labor?]" and "for eša 20 sìla per day [of female labor?]." What puzzles me is that, according to the first statement, eša flour would have double the value of dabin flour; while according to the second statement, twice the quantity of eša can be processed in the same time as dabin. Hence, one would assume that dabin has, at least from a labor point of view, twice the value as eša (in barley equivalents). I do not claim that there is

so important in an economy of regulated and manipulated values.

For several reasons, this account (Table 1) is particularly fascinating and may prove rewarding for the serious student of archaic bookkeeping. However, the reader must be warned that the rest of the current section and next section requires concentration and constant reference to the details shown in Table 1. A first glance at this table reveals that, in contrast to a modern work-in-process account, only the raw materials (upper part of the debit side) and the finished products (upper part of the credit side) are endowed with "values" (expressed in liters of barley equivalents — see second figure column; the first figure column indicates actual liters of the grain specified). The labor input is merely shown in "female labor days" (FLD, lower part of the account), but is not evaluated in barley equivalents. Furthermore, unlike the upper part, the lower debit side contains a *global budgeted* figure (plus an adjustment near the bottom), while the lower credit side shows *actual* FLD, detailed by type of work. Finally, the deficit (to be brought forward to the next period) on the lower credit side and the ultimate total (valued in equivalent barley liters) also exclude the labor contribution. From this we may conclude that the purpose of such accounting was mainly *stewardship*, not the determination of the "true" cost or value of goods.[11] The foreman's production account is charged with those amounts of grain he received from various sources or persons (Ir, Lugal-usur, and Nin-melam) for which he gave account on the credit side by showing what he had produced and distributed. The balance of these commodity values was shown as a *deficit* (or surplus) and, usually, carried forward to the next accounting period for settlement. To account for the labor days consumed, the foreman had to include

a contradiction here because it might be that, precisely because eša could be processed faster, it was more highly valued. Nevertheless, this seems strange and should be reevaluated.

[11]NDE [1993, figure 43 and the pertinent text, p. 51] presented a general schema of a "flow chart revealing the structure of the accounts . . . ," in which only the budgeted and actual labor days are taken into consideration, while neglecting the actual raw material input (dr.) as well as the output of finished products (cr.) based on actual (not on budgeted) data. If the raw material input would also have been on a budgeted basis, the actual input of those items would have to be shown somewhere in the account which, however, was not the case. This is surprising and contrary to NDE [1993, figure 69] where raw materials and finished goods, instead of labor, appeared to dominate the account.

in this account, as a kind of side calculation, a comparison of budgeted labor hours (dr.) with actual labor hours (cr.).

TABLE 1

The Author's Accounting Interpretation of Nissen et al., 1993, pp. 84-95.

See corrected **TABLE 1**

in subsequent paper:

"FOLLOW-UP TO: 'RECENT INSIGHTS INTO MESOPOTAMIAN ACCOUNTING OF THE 3RD MILLENNIUM B.C.'"

A further interesting aspect of this particular account is a recording procedure made necessary by the death of a female laborer during the budget period. As the FLD were budgeted in advance, though recorded *ex post* for comparison with actual data, the foreman was responsible for all the projected FLD of the deceased, even for days she could no longer work. Thus, after her demise, the remaining, but budgeted, 187 FLD had to be cancelled by a credit entry. Yet, this was complicated by the fact that each worker had a budgeted allowance for free days (for females, usually one-sixth of her total budgeted work). Hence, one-sixth of the 187 FLD had to be reversed by a debit entry. In referring to this example, NDE [1993, p. 88] emphasized that "no detail of this text exemplifies so drastically the high level of formalization achieved by bookkeeping of labor performance during the Ur III period."

UNEXPLAINED DISCREPANCIES AND OTHER ITEMS TO BE CLARIFIED

To balance the account in Table 1 in terms of barley equivalents,[12] I had to insert on the *debit side* an "unexplained discrepancy" of minus 2,000 liters. It results from the difference between the total of 92,618 liters (in the original: 308 gur, 3 barig, 3 bán, and 8 sìla) *minus* the sum total (94,618 liters) of the individual items listed on the top of this account. Although this discrepancy, not noted in NDE [1993], is merely slightly over two percent of the total, it would require clarification.

The upper half of the *credit side* shows an "unexplained discrepancy" of 60 liters (90,076 liters according to the total versus the 90,016 liters derived from adding the individual items — see upper credit side of Table 1 and NDE, 1993, p. 85). Furthermore, considerable discrepancies seem to exist with regard to "sig flour" and "ground bread" when comparing the individual items [NDE, 1993, p. 85, section II] with the totals (in its section IV) of these two products (55,905 liters of dabin flour and 16,349 liters sig flour, shown in the upper credit side of Table 1). Above all, the labor for excavation (270 FLD indicated in the lower part of the credit side of Table 1) seems to have, in contrast to the milling labor, no equivalent output data on the upper credit side of this Table 1 and its corresponding

---

[12]All amounts in Table 1 are rounded up or down to whole liters (sìla) of actual grain or barley equivalents.

data in NDE [1993, p. 85]. This movement of about 1,189 cubic meters of soil, 20.5 volume-šar per laborer, would correspond to a barley equivalent of about 200 liters, assuming minimum rations, that might have to be inserted on the upper credit side.

As to the lower part of Table 1, the accounting for labor appears to be proper on both sides of the clay tablet, including the correctly inserted discrepancy of 620 FLD, called "deficit" by NDE [1993]. However, that last point requires clarification. How can this discrepancy be a deficit if the actual female labor hours used, hence contained in the output, are less than the budgeted ones? It rather appears to be a "surplus" or, more expertly expressed, a "favorable budget variance." The confusion may have been due to something that may, indeed, be puzzling to archaeologists. In accounting with *actual* data, a loss (deficit) is balanced on the credit side when expenses (dr.) are larger than revenues (cr.). But in accounting with *estimated data* (budgeting, standard costing, etc.), a "deficit," more appropriately called "unfavorable variance," is balanced on the debit side, provided the budgeted amounts are recorded on the debit side and are larger than the actual amounts on the credit side. And since our account, Table 1, contains actual data in the *upper part* (different cereals and ingredients as input and different flour types as output) with budgeted data of FLD in the *lower part*, the "deficit" for the commodity data and the "favorable budget variance" for the labor hours have both to be balanced (i.e., separately inserted) on the credit side. No wonder that NDE [1993] took a favorable budget variance for a "deficit" (i.e., an unfavorable budget variance). But perhaps the term "LÁ+NI," translated by NDE [1993, p. 49] as "deficit," merely means "discrepancy;" but this only a language expert could decide.

There still is another problem to be resolved. As hinted at, the commodity deficit of 2,542 liters is a genuine deficit because it concerns the discrepancy between larger input values versus smaller output values in real terms. It was mentioned by NDE [1993, p. 85, figure 69] in the last section of the credit side and is shown in barley equivalents in Table 1. It constitutes the foreman's debt, be it because of inefficiency or embezzlement, vis-à-vis the state at the end of the accounting cycle. This deficit is brought forward to the next period for settlement. However, apart from the question why the actual labor hours used are not converted into equivalent barley units and added to the total input, as would be done in modern production accounts, a special dilemma arises. Since the production output (i.e., the various flour types milled) is evaluated in barley equivalents, this "value" should also include the labor input besides that of raw material. But if that were the case, this entire enterprise of milling flour would appear to have been an unprofitable affair as the value of raw material input alone, apart from labor input, already exceeds the value of the total output by some 2,542 liters of barley equivalents.

Might it be possible that the workers (or slaves) received their standard rations from the same production process without having been recorded? Given this situation, the total of those labor rations (which, as footnote 10 shows, were much lower than the labor/product conversion rates there indicated) would have to be added on the credit side as an additional output. Perhaps the budgeted amount (including the unexplained discrepancy and labor deficit), in addition to figuring out the budget variance and the commodity deficit (or surplus), fulfilled a second task; namely, implying (instead of actually recording) the output of labor rations consumed by the workers during the production process. If this was the case, there are no indications that NDE addressed this particular problem or considered the need for entering actual labor values on the upper part of the credit side. It is also possible that the fixed conversion ratios were so distorted, in comparison to potential free market values, that the finished products were "undervalued" relative to raw materials. But if the foremost goal of the Sumerians was stewardship and its monitoring, such a scheme might have accomplished this task regardless of manipulated values or "transfer prices." Nevertheless, all those unexplained items and problems show that further inquiry is necessary. This may indicate that archaeologists alone might not be able to discover and resolve the pertinent intricacies involved, and that accounting expertise could play a vital role in this kind of research.[13]

---

[13]An excellent illustration of archaeologists drawing advantageously on the expertise of other scientists is the recent discovery of details in brewing beer by the ancient Egyptians. The "beer of Nefertiti," as it is jokingly called, yielded its secrets only after chemists and brewing experts were called upon.

AGRICULTURAL ACCOUNTING: REAL ESTATE
AND ANIMAL HUSBANDRY

Apart from clay tablets manifesting the surveying and measurements of arable land, there exist tablets containing the management and bookkeeping of real estate, usually public fields. Some tablets show on the obverse side the amount of grain necessary for seeding the fields based on systematic economic planning or budgeting, while the reverse side contains the pertinent field area based on standardized measurement techniques or approximations. Sometimes these measures are accompanied by a name or title indicating tradesmen, scribes, fishermen, and other professions. One such tablet contains no less than 104 such "allotments" for seed grains, probably from a central public granary. In Lagash (ca. 2400 B.C.), for example, fields were either (1) the domain of the ruler, (2) allotted to public officials, or (3) leased to farmers. The pertinent tablets contain such details on agricultural cultivation as expenditures, yields, and property status ("current rights of disposition"). In the agricultural area, no less than in the previously discussed non-agricultural recording techniques, progress over time can be observed: "In the Ur III period, field administration was improved by better documentation of the results of surveying. From this period on, sketched plans of the fields were included with the documents, annotated with length measures and calculated area measures like a modern land register. Similar plans have been found referring to buildings and, in rudimentary form, even to entire cities" [NDE, 1993, p. 68].

Bookkeeping for animal husbandry (sheep, goats, bigger cattle, donkeys, and, occasionally, horses and pigs) was another crucial component of ancient agricultural accounting. Of special interest is the recording of the holding and the annual productivity of some of those animals. The accounting dealt not only with productivity in terms of the production of milk, cheese, wool, fleece or fur, and textiles, but even processed dung for building or heating material and the propagation of the animals themselves. One text, for example, reveals that one-third of the ewes lambed during the year. To account for all this, the tablets had to reveal the sex as well as the age of the various animals cared for by the herdsman named in the record. Some of these records are quite comprehensive and, occasionally, refer to thousands of animals. In budgeting the production of such agricultural products as dairy fat and

cheese, the number of cows in the care of a particular herdsman was the criterion for calculating the expected output:

> One unusual document preserved from the Ur III pe-
> riod discloses crucial information on the calculations
> carried out in connection with cattle breeding and the
> expected output of dairy products of that time (see fig.
> 76). In this document, the annual production of 'dairy
> fat' and 'cheese' are calculated over a period of ten
> years based on the hypothetical growth of a cattle herd
> consisting, at the beginning of that period, of four milk
> cows [NDE, 1993, p. 97].

FIGURE 4

Schema of Budgeting the Growth of a Cattle Herd and its Dairy Output during a Ten-Year Period

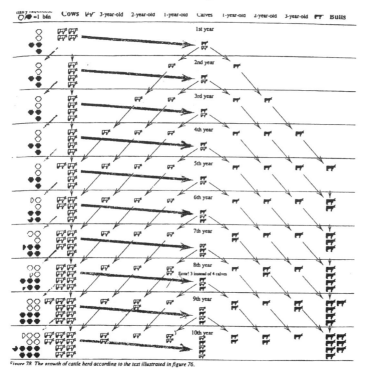

Figure 78 The growth of cattle herd according to the text illustrated in figure 76.

Source: Nissen et al., 1993, p. 101, Courtesy University of Chicago Press

Figure 4 offers the schematic-graphical presentation of a cuneiform tablet and illustrates the budgetary technique employed. It shows the anticipated development of a herd of cattle over a period of ten years. This tablet not only projects the growth of calves, cows, and bulls, but also the anticipated output of dairy fat and cheese from the first year (which starts with four cows on the left-hand side, but apparently with no bull until the fifth year) to the tenth year (which ends with ten cows and seven bulls; the latter indicated on the right-hand side). The left-hand side also shows the yearly expected output (in bán = ca. 10 liters) of dairy fat as well as cheese. Apart from the fact that the annual dairy production seems small from our modern point of view, it is surprising that no bull is recorded until the fifth year. As calves were produced in the first year, this was ostensibly with the aid of a "borrowed" bull, not revealed in the budget. The reader will also notice that, quite appropriately, the production of female and male calves is assumed to be equal over the entire decade, but not necessarily for each individual year. To maintain this long-term balance the sixth, seventh, eighth, and tenth years showed unequal numbers of male and female calves (see Figure 4).

A further tablet from Uruk III not only records on its reverse the total amounts of dairy fat (possibly butter or cream) and cheese, but converts these quantities into their equivalent silver values based on exchange rates such as 10 sìla (1 sìla = ca. 1.5 liters during the Old Sumerian period and about 1 liter during the Ur III period) of dairy fat per shekel of silver (1 shekel = ca. 8.3 g) and 150 sìla of cheese per shekel of silver.[14] This indicates that silver equivalents were occasionally used as an accounting or quasi-monetary unit (together with certain volumes of grain, animals, etc.) over four thousand years ago.

CONCLUSION

Historical research of early accounting and bookkeeping has brought forth a series of exciting and surprising results during the last two decades. Since SB's [1977, 1978, 1992] publications on this subject, we have been made aware of the ar-

---

[14]Note the difference in "price" or assigned value between cheese versus dairy fat (perhaps cream or butter) which, according to these ratios, would have been 1 to 15. Such a difference may seem to us extreme but was apparently appropriate in those times.

chaeological evidence of small clay tokens that were used by the peoples of the Fertile Crescent for recording the transfer of goods and the accumulations of debts or similar obligations from about 8000 B.C. to 3000 B.C. and occasionally later. The most decisive of these innovations was the idea to impress the tokens onto the outer surface of the clay envelope, the token content of which could thus easily be revealed without breaking the seals that identified the debtor and other features. This practice of "impressing" was antecedent to cuneiform writing, and constituted a particular kind of double-entry. Impressing the tokens on the surface of the container recorded, as an inseparable totality, a credit or ownership claim, while the inserting of those same tokens into the clay envelope recorded individually separable assets, including silver and claims to labor units, as charges. For a concise survey of token accounting, its evolution and discovery, see Mattessich [1995, pp. 23-32, figures 2.2 to 2.4].

Another decisive step, occurring in the late 4th millennium B.C., refers to the substitution of clay envelopes by more convenient flat clay tablets. At this stage clay tokens were merely impressed onto the tablet, indicating the individual goods and total debt owed, together with the appropriate seals revealing the debtor and possibly other information. Although the token shapes still continued for some time to represent types of commodities, this approach reduced the clay tokens from three-dimensional ideograms for commodities to *mere tools* for impressing two-dimensional ideograms. While the budding idea of a closed double-entry system as encountered in the token accounting of the 4th millennium B.C. disappeared, the legacy of debit/credit entries without systematic double-entry, as still found in some 20th century, single-entry accounting systems, was preserved in the archaic bookkeeping of the subsequent millennium.

The present paper dealing primarily with this legacy encountered in the proto-cuneiform and cuneiform record keeping of the 3rd millennium B.C. demonstrates the further development of early accounting into a relatively sophisticated system. In the late 4th and early 3rd millennia B.C., a transition seems to have taken place in which, increasingly, the form of the clay impression was determined by the commodity type in *combination* with a specific quantity of this commodity. Furthermore, some information about commodities and other data was incised instead of impressed and led, during the 3rd millennium, to proto-cuneiform and cuneiform writing. But beyond this development, which concerns more the history of writing, a series of important accounting innovations occurred. In the beginning of the 3rd millennium B.C., the practice of proto-cuneiform recording of commodity and labor transactions is characterized by placing the individual debit entries on the obverse side of the clay tablet while placing the sum total as a credit entry on the reverse side. This practice became less frequent during the late 3rd millennium B.C.; it might have been a residual from token accounting where individual tokens were put into hollow clay containers while those very tokens were impressed on the outer surface as the sum total of its content. From the middle of the 3rd millennium B.C. onwards, relatively sophisticated budgeting procedures with their *ex post* juxtaposition of budgeted amounts (particularly labor times) and actual data are encountered. If the stewardship function, between individuals or between them and a powerful temple administration, stood at the cradle of token accounting, this function became all the more important in times of centralized and highly bureaucratic governments. Therefore, the recording of a "surplus" or "deficit," the transfer of those balances to the subsequent period, and their ultimate settlement became a pivotal feature. This bureaucratization of economic life in the 3rd millennium B.C. (well known to the historically interested public through the names of such potentates as Mes-anni-padda, Sargon of Akkad, Gudea of Lagash, Ur-Nammu, etc.) was apparently the driving force for the development of more and more refined accounting and budgeting procedures, such as better calculation and surveying records, "transfer prices," and standard setting. Above all, the subsidiary information to the quantitative-numerical entries became much more sophisticated and semantically structured. The move from proto-cuneiform accounting to different stages of cuneiform accounting finally led to writing in general, and ultimately to literature and poetry.

A major incentive for discussing here crucial aspects of NDE [1993] is the fact that this book contains important evidence for conceiving new hypotheses and for strengthening those previously made [e.g., SB, 1983, 1992; Mattessich, 1987, 1994]. Such reinforcement is especially important in hypotheses that are not amenable to statistical testing. Another justification for this paper lies in novel insights concerning the Sumerian archaeology of accounting and some necessary reinterpretations beyond NDE [1993]. The challenge, be it to the archaeologists' or the accountants' traditional way of thinking, may be summarized as follows:

(1) This book and my paper present evidence that strengthens the hypothesis that *Sumerian token-envelope accounting of the 4th millennium* B.C. *is linked to the very different proto-cuneiform and cuneiform bookkeeping of the subsequent 3rd millennium* B.C. This link lies not merely in the acceptance of many results of SB's research in NDE [1993], but in a specific similarity between those two systems. It was originally hypothesized in Mattessich [1987, 1994] that (i) the inside of the envelope contains clay tokens representing individual assets, and (ii) that the *total* of these "asset values" is shown on the reverse; i.e., on the surface of the envelope, as a totality and equity in form of a set of inseparable token impressions. The similarity between this practice and proto-cuneiform or cuneiform bookkeeping is too striking to be coincidental. Those latter systems also carry on the obverse side individual entries as debits, while on the reverse side they carry the sum totals as credits, clearly evidenced in NDE [1993]. But this specific, yet decisive link between two very different debit-credit systems and its implication for the new hypothesis that *the way of making entries in "archaic bookkeeping" evolved directly from token accounting* are neither articulated in NDE [1993] nor in any other publication known to me.

(2) The above-mentioned evidence and hypothesis establishing the debit-credit character of both systems and their link, together with the fact that every token-envelope accounting can be considered a closed and self-contained system, reinforce the other previously made hypothesis [cf., Mattessich, 1987, pp. 80-81, 1994, pp. 18-21]; namely, that *token-envelope accounting constitutes a prototype of systematic (i.e., "closed") double-entry*, in which every entry has a counter-entry, and is not to be confused with a mere debit-credit system where only some but not all entries have a counter-entry.

(3) The preceding items, together with further evidence in NDE [1993] from proto-cuneiform and cuneiform bookkeeping, support and reinforce a third claim [cf., Mattessich, 1994, pp. 21-22]; namely, that those later record-keeping systems, despite having debit and credit features and showing occasional counter-entries, were not systematic double-entry systems. Here another pertinent difference to observe is that the counter-entries of token-envelope accounting represented

exclusively equity claims (either from debtors or owners, thus "closing" the system), while those of proto-cuneiform and cuneiform bookkeeping often represented transfer entries (outputs to other accounts).

(4) Furthermore, the paper translates (in Table 1) a fairly typical cuneiform account into a more conventional format, thereby revealing additional details as well as errors of interpretation, pardonable for archaeologists but important for accountants to observe. For example, what NDE [1993] called a "deficit" is, in one case, a "surplus" (or more precisely, a "favorable budget variance"). Also, the pertinent account contains, on several levels, "unexplained discrepancies" and deviates crucially from modern accounts in that it is a combination of a current account, of raw materials input and finished goods output, with a budget account, juxtaposing only labor input projections with actual output. None of those items were analyzed in the text of NDE [1993] which, therefore, requires some reinterpretation and further analysis.

(5) I hope this paper also dispels the conventional view that cuneiform record keeping was so primitive that such terms as "bookkeeping" and "accounting" cannot be properly applied to it. This misconception is compounded by the erroneous belief that accounting requires writing and abstract counting as prerequisites, as stated in conventional accounting texts [cf., Skinner, 1987]. Above all, this paper shows that accounting has deep cultural roots to be explored in cooperation with such subjects as archaeology. Should our discipline aspire to overcome its parochial tradition, then accountants ought to concern themselves with a broader range of knowledge and must take the effort to look at the pertinent research with a critical eye. Above all, those doing this work must convey their insights to the academic accounting community in general, not merely to specialized groups.

REFERENCES

Bernstein, Leonard (1976), *The Unanswered Question — Six Harvard Lectures* (Cambridge, MA: Harvard University Press).

Bram, Leon L., Phillips, Robert, and Dickey, Norma H. (eds.) (1979), *Funk & Wagnalls New Encyclopedia*, 27 Vols. (New York: Funk & Wagnalls, Inc.).

Mattessich, Richard (1987), "Prehistoric Accounting and the Problem of Representation: On Recent Archaeological Evidence of the Middle East from 8000 B.C. to 3000 B.C.," *Accounting Historians Journal*, Vol. 14, No. 2: 71-91.

Mattessich, Richard (1989), "Accounting and the Input-Output Principle in the Prehistoric and Ancient World," *Abacus*, Vol. 25, No. 2: 74-84.

Mattessich, Richard (1994), "Archaeology of Accounting and Schmandt-Besserat's Contribution," *Accounting, Business and Financial History*, Vol. 4, No. 1: 5-28.

Mattessich, Richard (1995), *Critique of Accounting — Examination of the Foundations and Normative Structure of an Applied Discipline* (Westport, CT: Quorum Books, Greenwood Publishing Group).

Melis, Federigo (1950), *Storia della Ragioneria* (Bologna: Dott. Cesare Zuffi, editore).

Nissen, H. J., Damerow, Peter, and Englund, R. K. (1993), *Archaic Bookkeeping — Early Writing Techniques of Economic Administration in the Ancient Near East* (Chicago, IL: University of Chicago Press), Paul Larsen (trans.).

Schmandt-Besserat, Denise (1977), "An Archaic Recording System and the Origin of Writing," *Syro-Mesopotamian Studies*, Vol. 1, No. 2: 1-32.

Schmandt-Besserat, Denise (1979), "Reckoning Before Writing," *Archaeology*, Vol. 32, No. 3: 23-31.

Schmandt-Besserat, Denise (1983), "Tokens and Counting," *Biblical Archaeologist*, Vol. 46: 117-120.

Schmandt-Besserat, Denise (1992), *Before Writing*, Vol. I, *From Counting to Cuneiform*; Vol. II, *A Catalogue of Near Eastern Tokens* (Austin, TX: University of Texas Press).

Skinner, Ross M. (1987), *Accounting Standards in Evolution* (Toronto, ON: Holt, Rinehart and Winston).

Vollmers, Gloria (1996), "The Persepolis Fortification Texts: Accounting and Control in Ancient Persia from 509 to 494 B.C.," *Accounting Enquiries*, Vol. 6: 1-43.

Accounting Historians Journal
Vol. 25, No. 2
December 1998

Richard Mattessich
UNIVERSITY OF BRITISH COLUMBIA

FOLLOW-UP TO: "RECENT INSIGHTS INTO MESOPOTAMIAN ACCOUNTING OF THE 3RD MILLENNIUM B.C.:" CORRECTION TO TABLE 1.

In the following, the corrected version of Table 1 to the above-mentioned paper [Mattessich, 1998] is shown. The author apologizes for having supplied (on p. 16) an obsolete version (based on incorrect conversion rates). In consequence, the figures of this table did not match with the figures of the first 17 lines of the commentary in the subsequent section, "UNEXPLAINED DISCREPANCIES AND OTHER ITEMS TO BE CLARIFIED" (p. 17). The present version does match this original commentary (a proof that two versions of the table got switched erroneously). However, I ask the reader to regard my interpretations of Nissen et al. [1993] as a preliminary attempt by an accountant, hardly familiar with the intricacies of Sumerian language and measurement systems. As was repeatedly hinted at, this area is worthy of continuing research.

The figures of the new Table 1 conform to the original conversion rates (for translating such Sumerian volume measures, such as gur, barig, bán and sìla, into each other and into liters) and to the conversions of various types of raw material and various finished products (types of flours) into their barley equivalents [for both types of conversion rates, see Mattessich, 1998, fn. 10, p. 14]. Above all, the new table matches with the commentary in Mattessich [1998, p. 17].[1] This commentary may require (on p. 17, four lines from the bottom) the insertion of the following addition after the expression "of Table 1):"

---

[1]For editorial reasons it was not possible to include here a reprint of the original table from Nissen et al. [1993, p. 85] of which my Table 1 is an "accounting interpretation." However, for the sake of checking and comparison, I intend to include a reproduction of the original table in the planned book [Mattessich, 1999] that is to contain, among other papers, Mattessich [1998], including the revised Table 1.

However, those discrepancies vanish if one takes the 10,755 liter (35 gur, 2 barig, 1 bán, 5 sìla) of "'pounded' flour" (listed in Section II, line 10) to be sig flour (which, perhaps, should have been emphasized in Nissen et al. [1993, p. 85]). This then has to be added to the 5,594 liter (18 gur, 3 barig, 1 bán, 4 sìla) in Section II, line 9. The sum of these two figures, 16,349 liter (sig flour) or 32,698 liter in barley equivalents, is the same as the corresponding figure (of 54 gur, 2 barig, 3 bán minus 1 sìla) shown in the total (of sig flour) in Section IV, line 7. As to "ground bread," there no longer seems to be any discrepancy between the individual listing (Section II, line 15) and its total (in Section IV, line 9).

REFERENCES

Mattessich, Richard (1998), "Recent Insights into Mesopotamian Accounting of the 3rd Millennium B.C. — Successor to Token Accounting," *Accounting Historians Journal*, Vol. 25, No. 1:1-27.

Mattessich, Richard (1999), *The Beginnings of Accounting Practice and Accounting Thought: Accounting Practice in the Middle East (from 8000 B.C. to 2000 B.C.) and Accounting Thought in India (300 B.C. and the Middle Ages)*, planned (New York: Garland Publishing Co., Inc.)

Nissen, H. J., Damerow, Peter, and Englund, R. K. (1993), *Archaic Bookkeeping — Early Writing Techniques of Economic Administration in the Ancient Near East* (Chicago, IL: University of Chicago Press), Paul Larsen (trans.).

TABLE 1

The Author's Accounting Interpretation of Nissen et al. 1993, pp. 84-93

Debit Side (in ltr.)		in barley equiv.	Credit Side (in ltr.)		in barley equiv.
Inputs/From Ir:			Produced and distributed:		
barley	59,925	59,925	dabin flour	55,905	55,905
emmer	11,400	11,400	sig flour	16,349	32,698
wheat	9,940	19,880	esa flour	701	1,402
From Lugal-usur:			fine gr.bread	44	11
barley	1,155	1,155			
spelt	525	1,050			
emmer	100	100			
From Bida: barley	900	900			
From Nin-melam:					
spelt	104	208			
Total in barley equiv.:		94,618	Total (in barley equivalents):		90,016
unexpl. discrepancy		(2,000)	**unexpl. discrepancy**		60
Total (from Nissen et al.)		92,618	*Total (from Nissen et al.)*		90,076

Budgeted Work (in FLD):		Actual Work (in FLD):	
Processing flour, etc.	11,304 FLD	Allow. for free time	1,884 FLD
		For flour filling	7,226 FLD
		For gr. bread	37 FLD
		For excav. work	280 FLD
		For winnowing barley	238 FLD
		For loading flour	30 FLD
		signed: Še-šani.	
		For carrying straw	19 FLD
		For other work	188 FLD
		signed: Šara-zame.	
		For bala(-service)	270 FLD
		For weaving mill work	96 FLD
		signed: ADU	
		For sieving flour	30 FLD
		signed: Ur-zu.	
		For ar<za>na fl. proc.	240 FLD
Allow. for free time of		Allowance for FLD of	
dec. lab. (1/6 of 187)	31 FLD	deceased labourer	187 FLD
		Actual. labour total	10,408 FLD
		unexpl. FLD-discrep.	304 FLD
		Total (according to	
Total adj. lab. budget	*11,335 FLD*	*Nissen et al.):*	10,715 FLD
		Lab. budget variance	620 FLD
		Deficit (to be br. forward in ltr.) 2,542	
Total (in ltr.)	92,618	**Total** (in ltr.)	92,618

Note: For lack of better information I have identified "sig" (top Cr-section) as "zì-sig$_{15}$" (which is double the barley value equivalents versus "ninda àr-ra-sig$_5$" which is only 1.5).

CHAPTER 6

Review and Extension of Bhattacharyya's *Modern Accounting Concepts in Kautilya's Arthaśāstra*

Review and extension of Bhattacharyya's *Modern Accounting Concepts in Kautilya's Arthaśāstra*

Richard Mattessich

Abstract

This is a discussion of the theoretical aspects of accounting as they emerged in India during the Maurya period (c. 321 BC to c. 184 BC) in Kautilya's *Arthaśāstra* (c. 300 BC) – the very first known treatise to deal with accounting aspects in the history of our discipline. Pertinent evidence can be found in an article by Choudhury (1982) and in Bhattacharyya's (1988) book, *Modern Accounting Concepts in Kautilya's Arthaśāstra*. This book, hardly known in Western accounting circles, claims that Kautilya's ancient treatise anticipated a series of 'modern' accounting concepts. These claims are here examined on the basis of the two standard translations of the *Arthaśāstra*, the original one by Shamasastry ([1915] 1967) and an extended one by Kangle (1963). Apart from some background material, the focus of this paper is on three aspects: (1) Kautilya's various types of income (including aspects of accounting for price changes, the distinction between real and fictitious holding gains, etc.) and their possible relation to modern concepts; (2) his classification of expenditures or costs (including possibly fixed vs variable costs); and (3) his notions of capital. These aspects indicate a surprisingly long-standing need for and possible use of relatively sophisticated accounting concepts. Thus Choudhury and, particularly, Battacharyya must be praised for drawing the attention of Western accountants to different aspects of an important ancient treatise. Yet Bhattacharyya (1988) deserves to be critically investigated and interpreted, not only from a Western point of view but also from the perspective of modern price-level accounting.

Keywords: accounting; history; India (third century BC); Maurya period; Kautilya

Accounting, Business and Financial History, Volume 8, Number 2, 1998
© 1998 Routledge 0958–5206

131

Introduction

Kautilya's *Arthaśāstra*[1] is little known to Western accountants or even accounting historians. It is not mentioned in standard accounting history books such as Littleton (1933), Chatfield (1974), ten Have (1986) nor is there any reference to it in pertinent anthologies, like Littleton and Yamey (1956), Edwards and Yamey (1994) or in theory texts that go back to ancient times, as does Most (1982). Only the recent encyclopaedic work by Chatfield and Vangermeersch (1996) refers to it briefly (though without mentioning Kautilya's name), stating that 'The first Indian Empire (325–150 BC) was ruled by the Mauryan dynasty. A book written during that time [apparently by Kautilya], the *Arthasastra*, described the political economy . . . There appears to have been a large and recognizable body of administrators, and offices for a treasurer, who kept accounts, and a chief collector, who was responsible for revenue records. The emperor sent officers on inspection every five years for an additional audit and check on provincial administration' (Vangermeersch, 1996: 325). But even the literature specializing on India (with a few exceptions) offers few details about the accounting aspects of the *Arthaśāstra*. Lall Nigam (1986), who tried, in vain, to show that Indian double-entry bookkeeping goes back thousands of years, is slightly more informative, but even he merely states that:

> The introduction and usage of a double-entry system of bookkeeping in India in times beyond the reach of historians is also evidenced by Kautilya's *Arth[a]sastra*, the oldest available treatise in political economy. The manuscript of this great work, dating as early as the 4th century B.C., contains a separate chapter on The Business of Keeping up Accounts in the Office of Accountants. . . . There are detailed references to the supervising and checking of accounts, and to the distinction between capital and revenue, expenses and profits. There are proforma summaries and tables relating to daily, monthly and yearly accounts [that] were prescribed, according to which the public accounts were to be presented. The accounts included estimates for the coming year (budgets) and the actual results of the year just ended (annual accounts). When the clerks of accounts attended with their books, the entire cabinet sat in conclave to scrutinize them and pronounce upon their accuracy, fullness and satisfactory nature in all respects. Kautilya cites various renowned authorities on the subject like Manu, Parashar, Narad, Shukracharya, Brahaspati and other sages. Even in the chapter on account-keeping, the various schools of thought are acknowledged in connection with the appropriate punishment to be meted to those responsible for any loss of revenue to the government.
>
> (Lall Nigam, 1986: 150)

Nobes (1987), who refuted Lall Nigam's claim as to the Indian origin of double-entry bookkeeping, mentions the *Arthaśāstra* fleetingly, but the paper by Scorgie and Nandy (1992) on 'Emerging evidence of early Indian accounting', despite its title, deals with a later period and does not mention it. Choudhury (1982) did devote an article to the accounting aspects of Kautilya's *Arthaśāstra*, though it is much less comprehensive than Bhattacharyya's (1988) hardly known book, touching – among other details – on important aspects involving price changes and their[2] profit and accounting implications. Thus, with the exception of Bhattacharyya (and to a lesser extent Choudury), other accounting historians seem to have missed the essence of the crucial accounting aspects of Kautilya's work. The situation might be different with respect to economic, social and political aspects to which this unique manuscript made interesting historical contributions as well; yet I could not find any reference, neither to Kautilya nor his Arthaśāstra, in such standard history works on economic thought as Einaudi (1953), Schumpeter (1954), Roll (1956), Fudaburk (1973), Hutchinson (1976), Creedy and O'Brien (1984), or the McGraw-Hill Encyclopedia of Economics (Greenwald 1994).

Let me first explain why I consider this ancient treatise of utmost importance. In the subsequent section I shall offer some background material and, above all, give you an indication of the suprising insights into accounting which Kautilya offered over 2300 years ago. If we compare, for example, Kautilya's Arthaśāstra with Pacioli's (1494) Summa di arithmetica, geometria, proportioni et proportionalita (in the following shortly called Summa), we first notice that both works deal mainly with matters beyond accounting (namely with politics, economics, finance and even war, in the former case, and mathematics, in the latter). But to the extent that these two works are concerned with our subject matter, one might say that Kautilya's pertinent sections deal with accounting problems – one is almost tempted to say with those problems in the modern sense, as Bhattacharyya (1988) claims –, while Pacioli's sections, as found in 'Particularis de computis et scripturis', are predominantly concerned with bookkeeping details. 'Accounting versus bookkeeping', this is a strong claim; but I shall put evidence before you to support it. Yet the mere possibility that insights concerning valuation problems, general and/or specific price changes, the need for different income concepts and holding gains, manifested itself long before the academization of accounting, should make us curious enough to learn more about Kautilya's Arthaśāstra. Indeed, everyone interested in the cultural mission of our subject matter cannot but get excited about such possibilities. The other amazing fact is, of course, that Kautilya's *Arthaśāstra* is some 1800 years older than Pacioli's *Summa*.

But why is Pacioli's work so well known in accounting circles while Kautilya's is shrouded in ignorance? First of all, Pacioli's work stands on the threshold of modern times and connects directly to the scientific-technological and 'capitalistic' *Weltanschauung* that constitutes our heritage. Above all, it is not a manifestation of an ancient and remote foreign culture. Yet, recently, accountants have begun to open their eyes to the importance of cultures beyond the horizon of Europe and America. It is dawning upon us that every truly cultural contribution (including those of accounting), wherever or whenever it may have occurred, is an enrichment of mankind. And, to paraphrase James Burke, how can we know where we are going if we do not know where we have already been? These are not just nice phrases but thoughts to which I shall give concrete content when comparing modern notions of changing prices and price-levels with insights gained some 2300 years ago.

Another reason for the insufficient regard to the *Arthaśāstra* by Western accountants might even have to be blamed on some Indian scholars and their writings. I do not intend to implicate authors like Lall Nigam (1986), but some might be tempted to do so by pointing out that he tried to relate the *Arthaśāstra* to his quite insufficiently substantiated claim that Indian double-entry bookkeeping (*Bahi-kata*) goes back thousands of years, and was finally imported to Europe by the Venetians.[3] It seems to me that the myopic concentration on double-entry bookkeeping, with the attendant neglect of deeper accounting issues, is the main reason why the true significance of Kautilya's work is still too much neglected. A further reason is the fact that Pacioli's work has continuously been known and revered for over 500 years, while Kautilya's was discovered or, rather, rediscovered only in 1905.[4] Before giving further accounting details of the *Arthaśāstra*, parallels may be drawn between Aristotle (384–322 BC), the renowned Greek philosopher and teacher of Alexander the Great, and Kautilya (fourth to third century BC),[5] the Indian sage and mentor of Chandragupta I. Kautilya helped to overthrow the Nanda family, placing the famous Chandragupta, first king (c. 321 BC – c. 297 BC) of the Maurya dynasty (occasionally addressed as emperor), on the throne of Maghada (now the area of Bihar).[6] Kautilya was a scholar of great theoretical as well as practical ability; his *Arthaśāstra*, written around 300 BC, consists of 150 chapters, and is by now a well-known ancient masterpiece containing not only commercial but foremost economic, ethical, legal, political and social thoughts and expositions One may even raise the question of why the *Arthaśāstra* concerns itself, at least to some extent, with accounting issues, while the even more comprehensive writings of Aristotle (despite revealing awareness of *economic* issues) are silent about accounting theory. As to their differing circumstances, it seems that Kautilya was closer to the centre of power insofar as his concern and advice pivots on the economic wellbeing of the state – so important for a ruler, like Chandragupta, who had to prove the superiority of his reign (particularly in comparison to that of his Nanda predecessors). And beyond that, according to Rao (1958: 19), the *Arthaśāstra* seems to have been 'an effort to reconstitute a decomposed social order, rudely shaken to its foundations by Hellenistic contacts'. Such considerations were of a much lesser concern to an Alexander the Great, whose relentlessly conquering war-machinery appeared to be the best guarantor of continuing power – at least during his lifetime. Thus, apart from the different interests of Kautilya and Aristotle, Alexander had little need to engage his mentor (who was thousands of miles away from those military campaigns) in promoting the economic welfare and taxation potential of an empire that was a conglomerate of many nations. Had those circumstances have been reversed, – who knows? – today we might be in possession of an Aristotelian treatise on accounting.[7]

Early accounting notions of ancient India

Although several publications by Indian and other authors mention the *Arthasāstra*, the only *book* doing justice to its crucial accounting aspects seems to be that by Bhattacharyya (1988), who was then working at the University of Calcutta. I have searched in vain for sources that refer to it. Yet, apart from the fact that it is hardly known (at least outside India), it requires critical evaluation, particularly from the point of view of up-to-date knowledge of price-level accounting.

Bhattacharyya submits evidence that a series of 'modern' accounting concepts were already used in ancient India, as early as the end of the fourth century BC when the *Arthasāstra* seems to have been written. Such a claim ought to be carefully examined and deserves to be interpreted from a rigorous point of view. According to Anil Mukherjee's foreword to Bhattacharyya's (1988) book, this is the first English commentary (with original passages in Sanskrit and their English translation) of Kautilya's thoughts on accounting. Actually, it is not clear whether Bhattacharyya used Sanskrit to translate those passages himself, or whether he had to lean on other sources in making his translation of selected passages. The first standard translation of the *Arthasāstra* is by Shamasastry ([1915] 1967); the second one (almost half a century later, supplemented by newly discovered fragments of the treatise and with more detailed commentaries) is by Kangle (1963).[8] In the limited space here available I have to forgo purely technical considerations, but will concentrate on what I consider to be the ancient Indian forerunners of major accounting concepts: notions that may, previously, have been deemed to belong exclusively to modern times. The following examples place the importance of Kautilya's contributions to 'theoretical' accounting into proper perspective, but also demonstrate the difficulties that arise due to alternative translations and interpretations. One passage of the *Arthasāstra* (though apparently not discussed in Bhattacharyya (1988) refers to a distinction that sounds similar to ours between *work in process, finished products* and *partly finished products*, as well as to our notions of *revenues, expenses* and *income* (net revenues) – even if subsequent passages refer to governmental accounting:

He shall also pay attention to the work in hand (karanīya), the work accomplished (siddham), part of work in hand (śesha), receipts, expenditure, and net balance.

(KA/II/VI/60; Shamasastry, [1915] 1967: 60)[9]

Another passage (from the same chapter, but item 61 – see Bhattacharyya, 1988: 16–17) points at a distinction of various types of 'income' (cf. also Kangle 1963: 91), but I prefer to quote below from Shamasastry's (1967) translation where the term 'receipts' is used instead of 'income'. This seems to make more sense in this context, at least from the point of view of modern accounting:[10]

Receipts may be (1) current, (2) last balance, and (3) accidental (anyajātha = received from external source).

What is received day after day is termed current (vartamāna).

What has been brought forward from year before last, whatever is in the hands of others, and whatever has changed hands is termed last balance (paryushita).

Whatever has been lost and forgotten (by others), fines levied from government servants, marginal revenue (pārśva), compensation levied for any damage (pārihīnikam), presentations to the king, the property of those who have fallen victims to epidemics (damaragatakasvam) leaving no sons, and treasure troves – all these constitute accidental receipts.

(KA/II/VI/61; Shamasastry, [1915] 1967: 60–1)

We can hardly expect, for these times or from translators, like Shamasastry or Kangle, who are not accountants, to make the proper distinction between the modern notions of revenues vs receipts, but we should at least try to discern the distinction between revenues (or receipts) and income. Thus I interpret the first two points of the last quotation as a distinction between *current revenues* and *deferred revenues* – to call this item 'accrued income', as does Bhattacharyya's text (or translation), makes little sense to me (can 'income' accrue, or can only revenues and expenses accrue?). The third category has the characteristics of our notion of *extraordinary items* (revenues from non-operational sources). This finds confirmation by Choudhury who states that: 'The balance (*nivi*) remaining after deducting total expenditure from total revenue (*samjātād āyavyayaviśuddhā*) was to be aggregated with the balance of the previous period and carried forward ... Thus it appears, from this and other definitions, that revenue and expenditure were to be accounted for on a receipts and payments basis (either in cash or in kind) without regard to accruals' (Choudhury, 1982: 107).

A definition of gain (or income) is found in the following passage: 'Likewise it is a loss to undertake a work of less output and of a greater outlay, while a work of reverse nature is a gain' (KA/VII/XII/301; Shamasastry, [1915] 1967: 332). This could be taken as a (round-about) definition of income and loss (as Bhattacharyya seems to do), and its logical extension could even lead to the notion of 'break-even point'. And the reference to '[c]ollection of arrears is termed "upasthāna," recovery of past arrears' (KA/II/XV/94; Shamasastry, [1915] 1967: 102), is interpreted quite reasonably by Bhattacharyya (1988: 19) as similar to 'recovery of Bad Debt previously written off'.

For me, one of the most fascinating passages of the *Arthaśāstra* is the following; due to its potential significance, I shall here present three translations of it:

> The profit due to rise in price of merchandise at the time of sale, sale of unsaleable goods and profit due to the use of different weights and measures is termed as Vyājī; the enhancement of price due to bidding among buyers is also another source of profit.
>
> (KA/II/VI; Bhattacharyya, 1988: 22)

> The rise in price of merchandise due to the use of different weights [footnote omitted] and measures in selling is termed vyājī; the enhacement [probably meaning 'enhancement'] of price due to bidding among buyers is also another source of profit.
>
> (KA/II/VI/61, Shamasastry, [1915] 1967: 61)

> Accretion, viz., increase in the price of commodities at the time of sale, excess in weights and measures called surcharge or the increase in price because of competition for purchase, – this is (also) income.
>
> (KA/II/VI; Kangle, 1963: 91, item 22)

In discussing Book II, Bhattacharyya, with reference to Chapter 27 (which deals mainly with 'Prostitutes' and their business), presents the following similar quote:

> if at the time of sale, the price of goods purchased earlier at a lower price rises, then, this sale will generate an *additional income.*
>
> (Bhatacharyya, 1988: 21)

However, I could not find and verify this passage in either Shamasastry's or Kangle's translation (perhaps the reference to the number of the book and/or chapter was incorrectly stated by Bhattacharyya). Yet, even without this last quote (and despite the fact that there are considerable differences in translation), all three translations of the preceding quotation indicate that we are dealing with an important accounting issue. These crucial passages not only manifest an awareness of general or specific price changes but also refer *explicitly* to potential profits accruing from those changes. In modern parlance one would speak of *fictitious holding gains* – which Bhattacharyya (1988: 22) seems to call 'unearned income' – in case of general price changes, but of *real holding gains* if specific price changes are referred to. Obviously, the passage distinguishes between at least two different notions of income or gain caused by price increases. But which one is meant by 'profit due to rise in price of merchandise at the time of sale' and which by 'enhancement of price due to bidding among buyers'? At this stage I am not prepared to answer this question, but I believe one cannot dismiss the possibility that one of them referred to specific and the other to general price changes.[11] Whatever the interpretation, Kautilya may have conceived over 2300 years ago at least some of the accounting implications of price changes. This should amaze every accountant, whether notions approaching those of modern inflation and current-value accounting were involved or not.

Further profit categories in the *Arthaśāstra*, such as profits from sub-standard goods or due to distorted weights, or from illegal goods, from unfair competition, etc., refer rather to ethical and fiscal considerations. Kautilya stipulates that such profits ought to revert to the government. One might interpret this and a host of other remarks on levies, etc., as an anticipation of tax accounting issues.

Expenses too are classified by Kautilya into various categories:

> Expenditure may be daily (fixed) expenses, daily extra (or, above the amount of fixed expenses) expenses, expenses for (or, to make) profit, and extra expenses for profit.
>
> What is spent every day is daily expenditure.
>
> What is spent during a fortnight, or a month, or a year is termed as (expenditure for) profit.
>
> Whatever is spent on these two heads (being more than the fixed or precalculated amounts) is termed as daily expenditure and profitable expenditure respectively.
>
> (KA/II/VI/presumably 61; Bhattacharyya, 1988: 26; again there are some discrepancies compared with Shamasastry's translation: 61)

Although the expressions in parentheses (within the translated text) seem to have been added by the translator, from the context it may be justifiable to conclude that Kautilya meant by 'daily expenditures' something like our *fixed costs*, while 'extra expenses for profit' seems to refer to *variable costs* in our sense. As to the remaining two notions, I find Bhattacharyya's commentary confusing, and suggest that Kautilya, who explicitly refers to the profit-making stage (likely to be stage of sales), might have referred to *fixed sales expenses* and *variable sales expenses*, respectively – while the first two categories may refer to production and/or administrative costs.

As far as the notion of *capital* is concerned, the following definition is offered:

> That which remains after deducting all the expenditure already incurred and excluding all revenue to be realised is the net balance or nīvī, which may have been either just realised or brought forward.
>
> (KA/II/VI/62; Bhattacharyya, 1988: 27; also Shamasastry, [1915] 1967: 61, with minor discrepancies)

Contrary to Bhattacharyya's view, the reader may find this an unusual definition of capital – it certainly does not conform to any of the six different definitions of this concept as listed by Cooper and Ijiri (1983: 82) in *Kohler's Dictionary for Accountants*. Nevertheless, it may be acceptable as corresponding to what nowadays is considered *ending capital* (even though it neglects characteristics of *beginning capital* or *capital* in general).[12] Particularly intriguing is the reference to capital 'realized or brought forward'. From a modern point of view this could mean that the capital notion containing only realized income (conforming to our nominal and real financial capital maintenance notions) was predominant. But what does net balance (i.e. capital) 'brought forward' mean? Could it not refer to capital including 'unrealized' income? If this were the case, then a capital corresponding to our physical capital maintenance notion would emerge as a possible alternative. But Bhattacharyya does not offer sufficient commentary to clarify this or other obscure points in the remaining text.

Furthermore, the *Arthaśāstra* (KA/II/X/71 in Shamasastry's translation) refers in several places to the notion of 'relevancy' which some might stretch as covering the modern accounting concept of *materiality*. Finally, Bhattacharyya (1988: 27–9), by referring to 'monetary cost concepts', points to the fact that Kautilya was dealing with an economy in which, beside barter, monetary transactions and monetary accounting notions played an important role. But this was hardly an innovation since money (introduced in Lydia some three hundred years before) had been widely used in Asia Minor, Greece and many other places since the sixth century BC. Yet the *Arthaśāstra* contains many passages that relate to further accounting and commercial concepts or, at least, suggests an awareness of issues leading to a series of modern concepts: for example, verification of receipts, expenditures, income, etc. (KA/II/VII/63–4), periodicity (of work paid for, and extra work; KA/II/VII/63)[13] long-term profit optimization (KA/II/XII/299 and KA/VII/IX/292), property loss (cattle) and recovery of property deemed lost (KA/II/XXIX/129), insurance against theft (KA/II/XXIX/129), production and sale of products and byproducts (KA/II/XXIX/130–1), sales tax (KA/II/XXIX/130), renting or leasing of property (KA/II/XXIX/128–9), duties of the village accountant and of district officers (KA/II/XXXV/142–3), etc.

Regrettably, Bhattacharyya repeatedly emphasizes that this or that notion is an 'Indian' and not a 'Western' concept. Although such ethnic pride is understandable in the light of the long suppression of a highly cultural nation, like India, by a Western power, these occasional remarks could be detrimental to the scientific purpose of his work. Bhattacharyya, for instance, remarks that: 'the author is firmly convinced that he has been able to establish the truth that the concepts of income, expenditure, capital, etc., and the practices of Accounting, Costing and Auditing were in vogue in ancient India and so, these concepts are not Western, but, basically Indian' (Bhattacharyya, 1988: xii). If one studies Sumerian accounting (cf.

Nissen *et al.*, 1993; Mattessich, 1998), one finds that notions such as
costing, auditing, periodicity and even income, expenditure or capital were
already deeply ingrained in ancient Mesopotamian commerce two thousand years or more before the Maurya dynasty of India. Even the recording
procedures of ancient Greece (preceding those of the Indian Maurya
Dynasty by more than a century) deal with accounts and such notions as
expenditures, revenues, capital, etc. (cf. De Ste. Croix 1956: 14–74). What
Bhattacharyya may have meant, but should have said explicitly, is that the
Arthaśāstra seems to be the first known, extant treatise that formulated
such concepts as income, expenditure, capital, etc., in a more or less clear
fashion. Such a crucial historical insight hints at achievements which
outweigh, by far, the dispute about which ethnic group or race has priority
status in the birth of early accounting concepts. To have drawn attention to
the fact that Kautilya's *Arthaśāstra* seems to be the very first treatise (as far
as we know) dealing with accounting notions more from a descriptive or
'theoretical' point of view than did the Sumarians, Babylonians, possibly
even the Chinese, seems to be the real merit of Bhattacharyya (1988).

It is also surprising that Bhattacharyya (1988) appears to have been
unaware of the more recent standard translation by Kangle (1963),
containing a host of commentaries in footnotes, as well as of the article by
Choudhury (1982). The latter, in a way, is proof against Mukherjee's (1988:
ix) belief that Bhattacharyya (1988) was the first to discuss accounting
aspects of Kautilya's *Arthaśāstra*. Further shortcomings of Bhattacharyya
(1988) are found in some of the interpretations and commentaries; these
often seem to stretch the imagination as far as the relation between modern
accounting practice and the text of the *Arthaśāstra* is concerned.
Occasionally, one might also question the terminology used in Bhattacharyya (1988); the terms may not always correspond to those used in modern
accounting theory. But the ultimate judgement on all those matters must
remain with future research.

Furthermore, there is the question of whether one may compare
accounting notions formulated some 2300 years ago, and under very
different social conditions, with those of our modern discipline, as done in
Bhattacharyya (1988). In this respect I should like to defend him. Above
all, I believe that whenever and wherever accounting issues, particularly
such as price changes and their consequences in profit measurement are
concerned, accounting is universal enough a discipline. I readily acknowl-
edge that different information goals require different accounting concepts, but I also believe that accounting possesses a basic core that is
timeless – though possibly not quite as universal as the concepts of the
physical sciences (which apply to extra-terrestrial phenomena and regions
as well). If a merchant or somebody else makes a profit due to the fact that
the sales price (of a commodity which he or she has held) has doubled, it
is a holding gain, whether today or a millennium ago. And if one has some
indication that this price change went beyond a more general or

inflationary price change, one had good reason to argue that this holding gain was at least partly a real one. And if that person did, indeed, sell this commodity, one may speak of a real as well as realized gain, whatever the social circumstances may have been or whatever terminology was used at the time. Such anticipation of some accounting notions is not dependent on disciplinary continuity. Of course, the latter cannot be assumed; and, if Bhattacharyya (1988) should deny this, I would have to distance myself from such a claim. But if a certain accounting notion existed in the mind of one or more persons 2300 years ago, and if this same notion appears thousands of years later in the form of a more formal concept, perhaps even within a different framework, it still is the same idea, independent of whether it continued uninterruptedly to exist in human minds or whether it was freshly conceived a thousand years later. In the latter case, I would find it all the more astonishing and worth proclaiming that such a notion was born a long time ago, even if dormant for ages. This holds for Hindu accounting concepts of the fourth and third century BC, no less than for much earlier accounting notions; for instance, those of the Sumerians of the third millennium BC and before (see, e.g. Mattessich, 1995: ch. 2, 1998). The major difference between the Hindu and the Sumerian notions is that the former are contained in a descriptive ('theoretical') text while the latter notions are primarily extracted from the Sumerian accounting systems themselves (i.e. from *representations* instead of *descriptions*). There too, *basic* accounting needs and notions, similar and comparable to ours in the twentieth century, manifested themselves in clear and indubitable records more than four thousand years old.

Apart from the items discussed above, Bhattacharyya (1988) contains other conceptual and many technical details (e.g. on preparing and designing accounts) which would warrant additional analysis. But, for the time being, this presentation has, hopefully, offered enough material to stimulate accountants (especially those familiar with Hindi or even Sanskrit) to undertake further research in this particular area, and to subject Bhattacharyya's (1988) praiseworthy effort to further scrutiny.

Auditing, taxation, financial and other aspects

Apart from Kautilya's surprising insights into basic accounting notions and some dimensions of accounting for changing prices, taxation aspects play a major role in the *Arthaśāstra*.[14] This is quite understandable; since early Sumerian and Babylonian times accounting has found its most ardent promoters among bureaucrats bent on securing and controlling revenues for temple and state authorities. Indeed, without the strong authoritarian government of Chandra Gupta, and its need to secure various taxation sources, it is unlikely that Kautilya would ever have incorporated any accounting considerations into his *Arthaśāstra*.

Book II offers sections on 'The Business of the Collection of Revenue by the Collector-General', 'The Business of Keeping Up Accounts in the Office and Accountants' and 'Detection of What is Embezzlement by Government Servants out of State Revenue', dealing with bookkeeping and auditing. There are specific references to the verification of receipts, expenditure, income or capital (KA/II/VII/63–4). The duties of village accountants and of the Collector General are described in KA/II/XXXV, while in KA/II/VIII no less than forty ways of embezzling are listed; and in the preceding chapter Kautilya considers the punishment of accountants and other officials for failing in their duties, be it by deliberate fraud or incompetence, negligence, etc. As to auditing proper, we find the following passage:[15]

> The receipt shall, on the Vyushta, the new year's day, be verified with reference to the place and time pertaining to them, the form of their collection (i.e. capital, share), the amount of the present and past produce, the person who has paid it, the person who caused its payment, the officer who fixed the amount payable, and the officer who received it. The expenditure shall, on the Vyusuta [should probably be Vyushta], or new year's day, be verified with reference to the cause of the profit from any source, in the place and time pertaining to each item, the amount payable, the amount paid, the person who ordered the collection, the person who remitted the same, the person who delivered it, and the person who finally received it.
>
> Likewise the net revenue shall on the Vyushta day be verified with reference to the place, time, and source pertaining to it, its standard of finesse [quality] and quantity, and the persons who are employed to guard the deposits and magazines (of grains, etc.).
>
> (KA/II/VII/64; Shamasastry, [1915] 1967: 64–5)

Much detail can be found on farm and cattle accounting (see KA/II/XXIX), though no mention seems to be made of such matters as income recognition ('realization') when a calf is born or at a later stage (e.g. when it is sold). Thus, the sophistication of Indian accounting for farms and animal husbandry, as expressed in the *Arthaśāstra*, does not seem to have much exceeded that which can be inferred from Mesopotamian accounts in the form of cuneiform clay tablets of the third millennium BC (see Nissen *et al.*, 1993: 89–104; Mattessich, 1998).

In Book III there are sections on the 'Recovery of Debts', prescribing various amounts of interest to be payed in different situations, etc. And numerous publications give evidence of Kautilya's interest in financial matters and taxation issues. Parmar (1987: 146–7), for example, comments on these aspects as follows:

> It is because of the meticulous care with which Kautilya deals with questions pertaining to finance that the *Arthaśāstra* is also known as a treatise on applied finance ... It has tremendous relevance to modern

times and is perhaps the only work of its kind in classical antiquity – unique, brilliant, objective and far-reaching ... Kautilya lays great emphasis on the importance of treasury and makes every effort to increase receipts and reduce expenditure. [p. 146] ... The term 'tax' did not mean the same thing in the Mauryan period as it means today. ... in ancient India, the relationship between the king and his people was one of contract. This relationship was so sacred that the subject was entitled to the refund of taxes if the state failed to protect him fully. ... Kautilya's theory of taxes was like the modern theory of prices, and prices were charged by a public authority for specific services rendered and commodities supplied. ... The field of taxation in the Kautilyan state was vast and all-embracing [p. 147].

Parmar (1987: 256–7) later refers to Kautilya's theory and system of taxation by stating that:

Kautilya's theory of taxation is governed by the norms of a surplus budget. Accordingly, Kautilya offers a comprehensive catalogue of items of revenue and expenditure, which demonstrates his systematic dealing with financial problems. In doing so, he has laid the foundation of sound financial structure. He devises an efficient mechanism for data collection and keeping of a complete record of accounts and census along with the statistics regarding history, occupation, income, expenditure, age and special characteristics of different sections of population ... [p. 256]. Kautilya's financial administration partakes of modernity insofar as it possesses the necessary attributes of budgeting such as fiscal year, estimates of expenditure and income, and statement of comparative estimates of receipts and expenditure of the preceding and the current year [p. 257].

Hence the activities of financial planning and budgeting also assume an important place in the *Arthaśāstra* (for further references see Parmar, 1987: 88, 166, 171–2).

Finally, Kautilya's *Arthaśāstra* is not merely significant for only for business accounting but also for government accounting; with some stretch of imagination it may even be regarded as a forerunner of national income accounting since the ultimate purpose of Kautilya's work was to strengthen the economy of the entire nation. Its significance lies in the attempt to offer accounting concepts of fairly general validity and to prescribe accounting rules or regulations to be adhered to in all sorts of entities (be it commercial, agricultural, governmental or, possibly, on a national scale). Of course, the very purpose of the *Arthaśāstra* pivots on governmental issues, but at this time governmental accounting and accounting for an entire nation would have been virtually the same – or, at least, the boundaries between the two were hardly established. This treatise may even be called in evidence for the close relationship between micro- and macro-accounting concepts. Choudhury is particularly prone to interpret the *Arthaśāstra* from a governmental and national income point of view:

> The state's aggregate revenue was classified by Kautilya in three different ways. First he had the "body" [footnote omitted] or "corpus" of income [footnote omitted], *āyaśarīram*, which identified the revenue with its seven sources. . . . Secondly, the total revenue was re-classified into seven "mouths" or "heads" of income, *āyamukham*, indicating the manner in which the revenue arose . . . The third classification consisted of "current income" (*vartamana*), "outstanding income" (*paryushta*) and "income derived from other sources (*anyajata*) [footnote omitted]'.

(Choudhury, 1982: 106)

In reading those passages one is reminded of the threefold categorization and measurement of social income (on the levels of input, distribution and output) customary during past decades. Thus one may see the significance of Kautilya's work in the fairly general validity of its concepts and of prescribing accounting rules or regulations to be adhered to by all sorts of entities (be they commercial or governmental).

Conclusion

This paper finds its justification in the fact that the accounting aspects of Kautilya's *Arthaśāstra* have been grossly neglected in the history of our subject matter, and in the need to draw attention to the subtle details and the profundity of this work. This neglect by accountants (and not only those of the 'West') is difficult to explain, but it is particularly surprising as the *Arthaśāstra* is the very first treatise on accounting, as far as present historical documentation goes. As far as I am aware, the only other publication discussing some aspects of it is an article by Choudhury (1982) which, however, is less comprehensive in discussing the accounting issues of Kautilya's *Arthaśāstra*. The small book by Bhattacharyya (1988) seems to be the first to have illuminated most of such details, but it is so little known that *The Book Review Index* (Cumulations 1988–95) shows not a single review of this book. Furthermore, Bhattacharyya (1988) is in urgent need of evaluation and detailed critical analysis. It is hoped that the present paper has offered such an analysis and opens the door to further pertinent investigations.

The following items summarize what I believe to be the essential and most important accounting aspects of Kautilya's *Arthaśāstra* and hence of the first known treatise dealing with accounting aspects from a more theoretical point of view than any previously known record on this subject matter:

1 It contains conceptual formulations (not merely the application) of such concepts as income and revenue, expenditures, expenses and costs, sales tax, capital, etc. Some of these notions (as well as some distinctions mentioned in the next item) are, of course, much older; some can be inferred from accounting *records* of Sumerian and Babylonian times (cf. Nissen *et al.*, 1993; Mattessich, 1995, 1998) but *not* from any theoretical discussions of these periods. Thus their theoretical presentation seems to occur, as far as historical documentation appears to go, first in the *Arthaśāstra*.

2 It manifests an awareness of such costing issues as work in process, partly finished products, and finished products, production of by-products, long-term profit optimization, insurance or risk distribution, renting or leasing, etc., and offers pertinent descriptions.

3 It offers discussion of verification, auditing and taxation procedures.

4 It refers to price changes and the different notions of profit or gain resulting from them, as well as the effect of these changes on accounting procedures.

The last item is probably the most important one in recognizing the *Arthaśāstra* as a treatise dealing with 'theoretical' accounting aspects and foreshadowing concepts that were systematically dealt with not before the twentieth century. These four items appear to be reason enough to put Kautilya's *Arthaśāstra* beside Pacioli's *Summa*, and revere both of them as the most crucial landmarks in the early history of our discipline. I also hope that accountants may be persuaded to read not merely *about* the *Arthaśāstra* but a complete translation itself, to form a personal appreciation of this ancient treasure trove.

University of British Columbia

Notes

This paper is based on my presentation 'Kautilya's *Arthaśāstra*, a Sanskrit treatise, formulating "modern" accounting issues some 2300 years ago' at the 20th Congress of the European Accounting Association (in Graz 1997). Financial support from the Social Sciences and Humanities Research Council of Canada is gratefully acknowledged.

1 The Hindi literature knows several ancient *Arthaśāstras* (a term that could literally be translated as 'wealth science' but probably is better regarded as 'scientific treatises' in general), but Kautilya's seems to be by far the most renowned one. In the following, *Arthaśāstra* always refers to that by Kautilya.

2 Occasionally it is claimed that the *Arthaśāstra* is too 'descriptive' and not sufficiently 'analytical' (Spengler, 1963: 228). This may be correct from our modern point of view, perhaps even in comparison with some works of Aristotle and other contemporary philosophers of Kautilya. But for accounting, the limitation to descriptive aspects hardly negates the theoretical nature of this

treatise, particularly in comparison to prior times. From those times we have but accounting *records* without much evidence of truly theoretical reflections about them.

3   See, for example, the refutations of Lall Nigam's (1986) view in Nobes (1987), Scorgie (1990), Scorgie and Nandy (1992).

4   Rao (1958: 1, 3) considers Shamasastry the discoverer of the *Arthaśāstra*: 'With the discovery of Kautilya's *Artha Sastra* by Dr. R. Shama Sastri in 1905, and its publication in 1914, much interest has been aroused in the history of ancient Indian political thought; [p. 1]. . . . The *Artha Sāstra* . . . is a compendium and a commentary on all the sciences of Polity that were existing in the time of Kautilya. It is a guidance to kings. . . . *Artha Sāstra* contains thirty-two paragraphical divisions [Books]. . . . with one hundred and fifty chapters, and the *Sāstra* is an illustration of a scientific approach to problems of politics, satisfying all the requirements and criteria of an exact science' [p. 3]. But going back to the preface of the standard work and translation by Shamasastry (1967: vi), it is revealed that the manuscript of Kautilya's *Arthaśāstra* was actually discovered by a person described merely as 'a Pandit of the Tanjore District' who handed it over 'to the Mysore Government Oriental Library' of which Shamasastry was the librarian.

5   Apart from spelling Kautilya, in some instances, as 'Kautilīya' (see Ritschl and Schetelich, 1973), he is occasionally referred to by his other names: 'The personal name of the author was possibly Vishnugupta, Chanakya the patronymic and Kautilya (or Kautalya) the name by which he was generally known' (Choudhary, 1971: 27).

6   Magadha (situated in the heart-land of India) was for many centuries one of the dominating Hindu kingdoms and cultural centres; it was also there that during the sixth century Gautama Buddha (the founder of Buddhism) as well as Jñātiputra Mahāvīra (the founder of Jainism) used to teach. Chandragupta I (called Sandracottus by the Greek) was the founder of the famous Maurya dynasty and empire (opposing further Greek invasion and, ultimately, in alliance with the Seleucid Empire) which lasted from c. 321 BC to 184 BC; it stretched from the Indus to the Ganges, and thus was the first Pan-Indian empire. Chandragupta's grandson was the even more renowned Emperor Asoka (c. 274–236 BC), whose conversion to Buddhism had widespread repercussions all over his country – dates, which vary from book to book, are taken from Langer's (1952) *Encyclopaedia of World History.* For a short description of Chandragupta and his mentor, let us listen to Durant (1954: 441):

> Chandragupta was a young Kshatriya noble exiled from Magadha by the ruling Nanda family, to which he was related. Helped by his subtle Machiavellian adviser, Kautilya Chanakya, the youth organized a small army, overcame the Macedonian garrisons, and declared India free. Then he advanced upon Pataliputra [the modern Patna], capital of the Magadha kingdom, fomented a revolution, seized the throne, and established that Mauryan Dynasty which was to rule Hindustan and Afghanistan for one hundred and thirty-seven years. Subordinating his courage to Kautilya's unscrupulous wisdom, Chandragupta soon made his government the most powerful then existing in the world. When Megasthenes came to Pataliputra as ambassador for Seleucus Nicator, [Greek] King of Syria, he was amazed to find a civilization which he described to the incredulous Greeks – still near their zenith – as entirely equal to their own. [Cf. Kohn (1929: 350)]

7   Further comparisons between Aristotle and Kautilya (who were about a generation apart) can be found in Rao (1958: 32–49).

8   There also exists a more recent version of Kautilya's *Arthaśāstra* by Rangarajan (1992) which, however, was not accessible to me.

9   'KA/II/VI/60' stands for 'Kautilya's *Arthaśāstra*/Book II/Chapter VI/Item 60'; the same convention is adhered to in subsequent citations. Bhattacharyya (1988) merely indicates the book and chapter (though *in reverse order*) but not the item. Kangle (1963) not only uses Arabic numerals to indicate the sequence of books and chapters but (due to incorporating fragments of the manuscript found at a later time, and for possibly other reasons) the numbering of 'items' is different (making his translation slightly more awkward to compare with those used by Shamasastry (1967) and Bhattacharyya (1988).

10 This seems to be in agreement with Choudhury's (1982: 107) interpretation of Shamasastry's translation 'If this was the meaning intended by Kautilya, then *nitya* and *lābha* may be paralleled with revenue [receipts] and capital expenditure.'

11 For details on the nature of various holding gains, their differences and combinations, see Mattessich (1995: 100–19).

12 However, Bhattacharyya (1988: 26) does state that: 'According to him [Kautilya], Capital is of two types: 1. Capital already deposited into the Royal Fund; 2. Capital remitted for deposit to the Royal Fund, but in transit.' The first item could be interpreted as 'beginning capital of a specific accounting period' while the second item as 'surplus added' to the beginning capital. Regrettably, Bhattacharyya does not indicate where (in the *Arthaśāstra*) the pertinent passage can be found.

13 Bhattacharyya's (1988: 15) translation of this passage is as follows: 'Three hundred and fifty four days and nights is a working year. Such work shall be paid for more or less in proportion to its quantity at the end of the month of Āshādha (about the middle of July). The extra work done during the intercalary month shall be separately calculated.' I think this confirms a certain notion of periodicity, at least as far as payroll accounting is concerned.

14 Reference to legalistic, administrative, financial and taxation aspects of the Arthaśāstra can, for instance, be found in Rao (1958: 171–222), Ramaswami (1962: 82–105), Choudhary (1971: 100–242), Metha and Thakkar (1980: 33–54), Parmar (1987: 53–201), Kumar (1989: 6–14, 27–31, 67–96). These books are all by Indian authors (written mainly in English, occasionally intermixed with Sanskrit passages). There also exists a treatise on the socio-economic aspects (of this period) in German by Ritchl and Schetelich (1973). Apart from the standard translations of the *Arthaśāstra*, the following commentaries deal with the Arthaśāstra and/or Kautilya: Aiyanger (1949), Bandhyopadhyaya (1927), Trautmann (1971), Mukherjee (1976), Narasingha (1985).

15 An appropriate supplement to this passage is the following remark by Choudhury:

> Annually, on the full moon day in the month of *Asādha* (around mid-July) the works officers and the accounts officers were to present themselves for audit at the *aksapatala* with sealed containers (of money and goods) and sealed books of accounts. To prevent any form of collusion these two types of officers would not be permitted to communicate with one another.
>
> (Choudhury, 1982: 108)

References

Aiyanger, R.V. (1949) *Indian Cameralism: A Survey of Some Aspects of Arthaśāstra*, Adyar: The Adyar Library.

Bandhyopadhyaya, N.C. (1927) *Kautilya: An Exposition of his Social Ideal and Political Theory*, 2 parts, Calcutta: R. Cambray.

Bhattacharyya, A.K. (1988) *Modern Accounting Concepts in Kautilya's Arthasāstra*, Calcutta: Firma KLM Private.

Chatfield, M. (1974) *A History of Accounting Thought*, Hindsdale, IL: Dryden Press.

Chatfield, M. and **Vangemeersch, R.** (eds) (1996) *The History of Accounting: An International Encyclopedia*, New York: Garland.

Choudhary, R. (1971) *Kautilya's Political Ideas and Institutions*, Varanasi: Chowkhama Sanskrit Series Office.

Choudhury, N. (1982) 'Aspects of accounting and internal control – India 4th century B.C.', *Accounting and Business Research*, 46(Spring): 105–10.

Cooper, W.W. and **Ijiri, Y.** (eds) (1983) *Kohler's Dictionary for Accountants*, Englewood Cliffs, NJ: Prentice-Hall.

Creedy, J. and **O'Brien, D.P.** (eds) (1984) *Economic Analysis in Historical Perspective*, London: Butterworths.

De Ste. Croix, G.E.M. (1956) 'Greek and Roman accounts', in Littleton, A.C. and Yamey, B.S. (eds) *Studies in the History of Accounting*, Homewood, IL: Richard D. Irwin, pp. 14–74.

Durant, W. (1954) *The Story of Civilization, Part I: Our Oriental Heritage*, New York: Simon & Schuster, first edition 1939.

Edwards, J. and **Yamey, B.S.** (eds) (1994) *From Clay Tokens to Fukushiki-Boki: Record Keeping Over Ten Millennia*, special issue of *Accounting, Business and Financial History*, 4(1).

Einaudi, L. (1953) *Saggi bibliographici e storici intorno alle dottrine economiche*, Roma: Edizioni di Storia e Letteratura.

Fudaburk, E.L. (1973) *Development of Economic Thought and Analysis*, Metuchen, NJ: Scarecrow Press.

Hutchinson, W.K. (1976) *History of Economic Analysis: A Guide to Information Sources*, Detroit, MI: Gale Research.

Geisbeek, J.B. (1914) *Ancient Double-Entry Bookkeeping*, Houston, TX: reprint edition by Scholars Book Co., 1974.

Greenwald, D. (ed.) (1994) *The McGraw-Hill Encyclopedia of Economics*, New York: McGraw-Hill.

Kangle, R.P. (1960) *The Kautilya Arthasāstra, Part I, A Critical (Sanskrit) Edition with a Glossary*, Bombay: University of Bombay, 1969.

Kangle, R.P. (1963) *The Kautilya Arthasāstra, Part II, An English Translation with Critical and Explanatory Notes*, Bombay: University of Bombay, 1972.

Kangle, R.P. (1965) *The Kautilya Arthasāstra, Part III, A Study [in English]*, Bombay: University of Bombay.

Kautilya, V. (c. 300 BC) *Arthasāstra*, India.

Kohn, H. (1929) *History of Nationalism in the East*, New York.

Kumar, P. (1989) *Kautilya Arthasāstra: An Appraisal*, Delhi: Nag.

Lall Nigam, B.M. (1986) 'Bahi-Khata: the pre-Pacioli Indian double-entry system of bookkeeping', *Abacus*, 22(2): 148–62.

Langer, W.L. (ed.) (1952) *An Encyclopedia of World History*, revised edn, Cambridge, MA: The Riverside Press.

Littleton, A.C. (1933) *Accounting Evolution to 1900*, New York: American Institute Publishing; reissue of first edition, New York: Russell & Russell, 1966.

Littleton, A.C. and **Yamey, B.S.** (eds) (1956) *Studies in the History of Accounting*, Homewood, IL: R.D. Irwin.

Mattessich, R. (1995) *Critique of Accounting: Examination of the Foundations and Normative Structure of an Applied Discipline*, Westport, CT: Quorum Books.

Mattessich, R. (1998) Recent insights into Mesopotamian accounting of the 3rd millenium BC – Successor to token accounting', *Accounting Historians JournaL*, 25 (scheduled for June).
Most, K. (1982) *Accounting Theory*, Columbus, OH: Grid.
Mukherjee, A. (1976) *Kautilya's Concept of Diplomacy: A New Interpretation*, Calcutta: Minerva Associates.
Mukherjee, A, (1988) 'Foreword', in Bhattacharyya, A.K., *Modern Accounting Concepts in Kautilya's Arthaśāstra*, Calcutta: Firma KLM Private, pp. ix–x.
Narasingha, P.S.I. (1985) *Kautilya's Arthaśāstra: A Comparative Study*, Calcutta: Academic Publishers.
Nissen, H.J., Damerow, P. and Englund, R.K. (1993) *Archaic Bookkeeping: Early Writing and Techniques of Economic Administration in the Ancient Near East*, Chicago, IL: The University of Chicago Press.
Nobes, C.W. (1987) 'The pre-Pacioli Indian double-entry system of bookkeeping: a commentary', *Abacus*, 23(September): 182–4.
Pacioli, L. (1494) *Summa de arithmetica, geometria, proportioni et proportionalita*, Venice.
Parmar, A. (1987) *Techniques of Statecraft: A Study of Kautilya's Arthaśāstra*, Delhi: Atma Ram.
Ramaswami, T.N. (1962) *Essentials of Indian Statecraft: Kautilya's Arthasastra for Contemporary Readers*, London: Asia Publishing House.
Rangarajan, L.N. (ed.) (1992) *Kautilya: The Arthaśāstra*, New Delhi: Penguin.
Rao, K. (1958) *Studies in Kautilya*, 2nd edn, Delhi: Munshi Ram Manohra Lal.
Ritschl, E. and Schetelich, M. (1973) *Studien zum Kautiliya Arthaśāstra*, Berlin: Akademie-Verlag.
Roll, E. (1956) *A History of Economic Thought*, 4th edn, Englewood Cliffs, NJ: Prentice-Hall.
Schumpeter, J.A. (1954) *History of Economic Analysis*, New York: Oxford University Press.
Scorgie, M.E. (1990) 'Indian imitation or invention of cash-book and algebraic double-entry', *Abacus*, 26(1): 63–70.
Scorgie, Michael E. and Nandy, S.C. (1992) 'Emerging evidence of early Indian accounting', *Abacus*, 28(March): 88–97.
Shamasastry, R. ([1915] 1967) *Kautilya's Arthaśāstra*, 8th edn, trans. Mahamahopadhyay, Arthasadravisarada, Vidyalakara, Panditaraja, with an introductory note by Fleet, J.F., Mysore: Mysore Printing and Publishing House; 1st edn 1915, 3rd ed 1929.
Spengler, J.J. (1963) 'Arthaśāstra economics', in Braibanti, R. and Spengler, J.J. (eds) *Administration and Economic Development in India*, Durham, NC: Duke University Press.
ten Have, O. (1986) *The History of Accountancy*, 2nd edn, trans. van Seventer, A., Palo Alto, CA: Bay Books; first edn 1976; original version *De geschiednis van het boekhouden in vogelflucht*, Holland, 1972.
Trautmann, T. (1971) *Kautilya and the Arthaśāstra: A Statistical Investigation of the Authorship and Evolution of the Text*, Leiden: E.J. Brill.
Vangermeersch, R. (1996) 'India (600 B.C. – A.D. 1856),' in Chatfield, M. and Vangermeersch, R. (eds) *The History of Accounting; An International Encyclopedia*, New York: Garland Publishing, p. 325.

CHAPTER 7

From Accounting to Negative Numbers

A Signal Contribution of Medieval India to Mathematics

Accounting Historians Journal
Vol. 25, No. 2
December 1998

Richard Mattessich
UNIVERSITY OF BRITISH COLUMBIA

FROM ACCOUNTING TO NEGATIVE NUMBERS: A SIGNAL CONTRIBUTION OF MEDIEVAL INDIA TO MATHEMATICS

Abstract: The major object of this paper is to present evidence for arguing that the highly developed Hindu accounting tradition, beginning with Kautilya's *Arthaśāstra* about 300 B.C., or even earlier, may have had a part in the more receptive attitude of medieval Indian mathematicians, compared to Europeans, in accepting negative numbers. The Hindus justified this attitude by arguing that having a debt is the inverse of possessing an asset; thus, attributing a negative number to a debt but a positive one to an asset. To advance the argument, the paper shows that the accounting aspect of debt is at least as basic as its legalistic one. Indeed, the former can be traced to the 4th millennium B.C. or earlier, while the first known legal codes go back only to the 3rd millennium B.C. However, there are other angles from which to examine the relation between accounting and negative numbers. Some accountants [e.g., Peters and Emery, 1978] believe that the long-standing hesitation of European mathematicians to accept negative numbers contributed to the accountants' debit/credit scheme, while others [e.g, Scorgie, 1989] deny this view. But this controversy concerns rather the influence of negative numbers upon accounting. It neglects to investigate the reverse possibility; namely, the influence of accounting upon the Indian mathematicians' early acceptance of negative numbers. Thus, this paper first reviews concisely, for the sake of contrast, the arguments between Peters and Emery [1978] and Scorgie [1989]; then it elaborates on the long-standing resistance of Western mathematicians to legitimizing negative numbers (which, in its entirety, did not happen before the 19th century); and, finally, it discusses the very different attitude of medieval Indian mathematicians, who were the first to accept negative magnitudes as numbers (e.g., Brahmagupta, 7th century A.D., Bhāskara, 12th century A.D.). Their interpretation of a negative number as representing "debt" as a basic accounting and legal notion may have been conditioned by the long-standing accounting tradition of India since the 3rd century B.C. or before.

Acknowledgments: Financial support from the Social Sciences and Humanities Research Council of Canada for this paper is gratefully acknowledged. I also want to express my thanks to the editorial team, including two reviewers and the editor, for valuable advice and stimulating my thoughts.

Submitted May 1997
Revised June 1997
Accepted October 1997

Probing more deeply into mathematical history shows that accounting aspects may have played an important role in medieval India through the earliest acceptance of negative numbers. This deserves at least as much attention as did the controversy between Peters and Emery [1978] and Scorgie [1989] as to whether or not the avoidance of negative numbers by Western mathematicians influenced the development of double-entry bookkeeping in Renaissance Europe. Peters and Emery [1978] tried to show that due to the rejection of negative numbers by Renaissance mathematicians, account balances had to be kept positive; e.g., relying on the "basic balance sheet equation" A = L + OE, instead of A - L = OE. One might counter this argument by pointing out that the balance sheet equation (A = L + OE) is more likely to have resulted from entering every transaction twice, and on opposite sides, via the trial balance because mathematicians and even accountants of this time were already sophisticated enough to know that the equation A - L = OE is an equivalent transposition of A = L + OE. But neither of these equations, nor a balance sheet, are mentioned in Pacioli's *Summa* [1494]. There one encounters merely the Profit and Loss account and the trial balance as well as the inventory, which also served as a starting basis for opening the accounts, thus approaching the notion of balance sheet. This "need for a bookkeeping system free of negative balances," in turn, was supposed to have led in commerce and in Fra Luca Pacioli's *Summa* [1494] to the notions of debits (Per) and credits (A) instead of regarding the values of assets as positive and those of all equities as negative. Scorgie [1989], quite correctly, refuted such an interpretation by pointing out the following three "critical evidential errors" contained in the argument by Peters and Emery:

(1) Omar Khayyám's (ca. 1048 - ca. 1131) rejection of negative numbers, introduced in India by Brahmagupta, b. 598, was supposed to indicate that the use of negative numbers "died out in India," if it really did at that time. Scorgie [1989, p. 317] claimed this to be invalid because a comment contained in Colebrooke [1973, p. iii], accompanying his translation of Brahmagupta together with that of Bhāskara II (b. 1115, Bhāskara hereafter), demonstrated that the work of the latter "was in the hands of both Mahammedans and Hindus between two and three centuries ago."

(2) Peters and Emery's [1978, p. 425] assertion, claimed to be based on Cajori [1919, p. 107], that "the Arabs also rejected negative numbers, in spite of knowledge of their use in India"

was shown to be invalid by Scorgie [1989, p. 317] because Cajori referred to the mathematician Abu'l-Wafa (b. 940) who authored a text that "termed the result of the subtraction of the number 10 - 5 [which is 5] from 3 a 'debt (dayn) of 2'" as quoted from Youschkevitch [1970, Vol. 1, p. 41]. Scorgie also referenced Vogel [1970, Vol. 4, p. 611], who pointed out that Leonardo Pisano (Leonardo da Pisa, also called Fibonacci, c. 1170-1250) "recognizes negative quantities and even zero as numbers."[1]

(3) Peters and Emery's [1978, p. 426] further assertion, that "there is no question that Pacioli rejected negative numbers" was called "nonsense" by Scorgie [1989, p. 318] because Pacioli [1494, ff. 114 v.-115 r.] stated 12 rules for subtraction with an example of subtracting 16 from 4 which gives a pure negative number called by Pacioli [1494, f. 114 v.] "puro meno."[2]

As the argument between Peters and Emery, on one side, and Scorgie, on the other, related accounting to negative numbers, it creates an inverse parallel to the main objective of this paper, thus offering a contrasting background as well as "counterpoint."[3] This objective lies in the search for evidence supporting the hypothesis that the highly developed Hindu accounting

---

[1]But the reader should note: "Rather surprising is the fact that Al-Karkhi's algebra shows no traces whatever of Hindu indeterminate analysis. But most astonishing it is, that an arithmetic by the same author completely excludes the Hindu numerals. It is constructed wholly after Greek pattern. Abu'l-Wefa, also, in the second half of the 10th century, wrote an arithmetic in which Hindu numerals find no place. This practice is the very opposite to that of other Arabian authors" [Cajori, 1919, pp. 106-107]. The last sentence shows that, again, Peters and Emery [1978] seemed to have misread their source.

[2]Apart from my agreement with Scorgie [1989], two aspects may have to be added. First, the essence of double-entry bookkeeping goes beyond the mere interpretation of assets as positive and debts as negative; it assigns a *negative* number also to an output of an asset and, inversely, a *positive* number to a reduction of a debt or ownership claim. Second, and more importantly, a mere debit/credit scheme as, for example, employed in a "charge-and-discharge statement" [see Cooper and Ijiri, 1983, p. 95], still lacks the pivotal feature of a closed double-entry system and can hardly be regarded as such.

[3]Critics may argue that this short discussion of the papers by Peters and Emery [1978] and Scorgie [1989] is not warranted here. But just as some music fans are only interested in rhythm or a single melody, others listen no less to harmony and *counterpoint*. Similarly, I presume the readers of *AHJ* are interested not merely in one aspect but in the entire picture from which this paper evolved. After all, the above-mentioned papers dealt also with the relation between accounting and negative numbers and provided an impetus for writing this article.

tradition, beginning with Kautilya's *Arthaśāstra* about 300 B.C. or even earlier, may have had a part in the earliest acceptance or legitimization of negative numbers by mathematicians. The latter happened in India during medieval times [Brahmagupta, 7th century, Bhāskara, 12th century — see translations by Colebrooke, 1973]. But to understand the long-lasting resistance of Western mathematicians to negative numbers, it is necessary to provide in the next section an overview of this particular development. Only then, in the third section, is it possible to discuss and appreciate the Indian achievement in its relation to accounting.

THE MATHEMATICIANS' CONUNDRUM WITH NEGATIVE NUMBERS

In relating negative numbers to accounting, or vice versa, it must be noted that the status of negative numbers in mathematics from ancient times to the 19th century experienced many twists and turns in the West as well as in the Orient.[4] This development was not as straightforward as one might believe from reading Peters and Emery [1978] or even Scorgie [1989]. Despite my agreement with the latter's objections to Peters and Emery, from a more global-historical point of view, the different attitude of Indians to negative numbers as well as to accounting ought to be considered. Thus, this paper shows, among other things, that in medieval India the important connection between negative numbers in mathematics and the debtor-creditor aspects of bookkeeping point in the direction from the latter to the former rather than vice versa. If historians of mathematics found this worth remarking, then accountants should be even more interested because it confirms the wide cultural impact of accountability notions. To recognize this, two insights, formulated in the third section as auxiliary hypotheses, are necessary — (i) a debt relation is not merely a legalistic but also a basic accounting concept, and (ii) debt relations and many other basic accounting notions were conceived and described, not merely used, in India long before medieval times, thus establishing an early and relatively advanced accounting tradition.

---

[4]An example of varying attitudes in Asia toward negative magnitudes is, on one side, the acceptance of negative numbers by such leading mathematicians as Brahmagupta (7th century) and Bhāskara (12th century), while other Oriental scholars (e.g., many Arabs — see footnote 2), possibly even the Persian poet and astronomer Omar Khayyám *may have* rejected negative numbers.

The earliest records of negative numbers, as Peters and Emery [1978, p. 425] mentioned, point to the Chinese, particularly to the mathematician Sun-Tsu [see *Sun-Tsu Suan-ching* or *Arithmetical Classic of Sun-Tsu*, 1st century], who not only presented different mathematical units by different positions and combinations of rods, but also distinguished positive numbers by using red rods and negative numbers by black rods [cf. Cajori, 1919, p. 72].[5] But the statement by Peters and Emery [1978, p. 425] that, "according to Cajori [1919, p. 72], the earliest reference to negative numbers is found not in mathematics, but, surprisingly, in commerce," is a puzzling misinterpretation as *Sun-Tsu Suan-ching* is undoubtedly a mathematical work. Above all, there is no pertinent reference in Cajori [1919, pp. 71-73] to commerce, merely to a possible derivation of this practice from the red and black beads of the abacus, which also is a *mathematical* device. According to Boyer [1989, p. 227]:

The idea of negative numbers seems not to have occasioned much difficulty for the Chinese since they were accustomed to calculating with two sets of rods — a red set for positive coefficients and a black set for negatives. Nevertheless, they did not accept the notion that a negative number might be a solution of an equation.

Thus, even if the Chinese used negative numbers, the mathematical status of those numbers need not have been much higher than it was in ancient Greece. Even Cajori [1919, p. 93] agreed that the "Indians were the first to recognize the existence of absolutely negative quantities."[6] Thus, it is generally

---

[5]Of course, negative numbers must not be confused with the *operation sign* for subtraction; indeed, an ideogram for *minus* can already be encountered in ancient Babylonia; i.e., thousands of years before the earliest known use of a negative number as a *magnitude*. Or as Kline [1980, p. 116] pointed out, "Both Girard and Harriot used the minus sign for the operation of subtraction and for negative numbers, though separate symbols should be used because a negative number is an independent concept whereas subtraction is an operation." This reference refers to Albert Girard (1595-1632) [1629] and Thomas Harriot (1560-1621) [1631].

[6]Cajori's [1919, p. 93] expression "absolutely negative quantities" might refer to the recognition and treatment of negative quantities as genuine numbers; i.e., as those "equally important" to any other numbers presently known and in the future to be recognized. He may even have referred to the belief that reality itself possesses negative quantities, representable through negative numbers, etc.

The above qualification, "presently known and in the future to be recognized," may indicate that the legitimization of negative numbers in medieval

acknowledged that the first known use and legitimization of negative numbers *in mathematics* is in Brahmagupta's *Brahma-Sphuta-Sidd'hánta* [628, partly translated and commented on, together with some work by Bhāskara, in Colebrooke, 1973].[7]

But why did negative numbers come so late to be *generally* accepted in European mathematics? In a way, our number system goes back to ancient Greece where the *natural numbers* (i.e., the positive integers, such as 1, 2, 3, . . . etc.) formed an almost sacred basis. The Pythagoreans deemed the phenomena of the universe to be reducible to those whole positive numbers or their ratios. In refining their notions, they may have come to regard numbers in a more abstract way, but for them and other ancient Greek mathematicians, a number was always something *positive.* Even when such notions as the square root of 2 or the notion of π (i.e., the non-ratios, or what we today call the *irrational* numbers) were discovered, the Greeks refused to con-

---

India did not require knowledge of the entire gamut of our modern number system, from natural numbers to complex numbers or even transfinite ones. For medieval European mathematics, it would have been an immense step forward had its disciples accepted negative and irrational numbers in the same way as they accepted natural numbers and fractions.

For the reader interested in the achievements of eastern vs. western mathematicians in other areas of the number system, I refer to the internationally known text by Aleksandrov et al. [1963] which stated that "the concept of an irrational number simply did not originate among them [i.e., the Greeks]. This step was taken at a later period by the mathematicians of the East" [pp. 26-27]. "The Greeks discovered irrational magnitudes but considered them geometrically, as linear segments. . . . In this way the Greeks were already in possession of much of the material of contemporary elementary algebra but not, however, of the following essential elements: negative numbers and zero, irrational numbers abstracted entirely from geometry, and finally a well-developed system of literal symbols. It is true that Diophantus made use of literal symbols for the unknown quantity and its powers....but his algebraic equations were still written with concrete numbers" [p. 37]. Furthermore: "Omar Khayyam (about 1048-1122), and also the Azerbaijanian, Nasireddin Tsui (1201-1274), clearly showed that every ratio of magnitudes, whether commensurable or incommensurable, may be called a number; in their work we find the same general definition of number, both rational and irrational. . . . The magnitude of these achievements becomes particularly clear when we recall that complete recognition of negative and irrational numbers was attained by European mathematicians only very slowly, even after the beginning of the Renaissance of mathematics in Europe" [p. 39]. This last quote might possibly contradict what Peters and Emery [1978] assumed to be Omar Khayyám's attitude toward negative numbers.

[7]In Colebrooke [1973], Brahmagupta is spelled as "Brahmegupta'" and Bhāskara II as "Bháscara." But here we shall adhere to what seem to be the more common notations.

sider them as numbers. The Greeks "never succeeded in uniting the notions of numbers and magnitudes, e.g., dots on a continuous line. The term 'number' was used by them in a restricted sense. What we call irrational numbers was not included under this notion. Not even rational fractions were called numbers" [Cajori, 1919, p. 22]. Since that time, every step of extending the number system, be it in the direction of the full-fledged integer system, rational numbers, and even real and complex numbers, constituted a very uneven and mixed "progression." Surprisingly enough, one of the last categories to be generally accepted by European mathematicians was that of *negative* numbers, even though from the 13th century until the second half of the 19th century, some aspects of negative magnitudes were at certain times accepted by some eminent European mathematicians.

Negative numbers became known in Europe via the Arabs and Leonardo da Pisa [e.g., his well-known *Liber Abaci*, 1202]. According to Cholerus [1944, p. 143], Leonardo da Pisa is said "to have accepted negative solutions of equations, and remarked that the solution would be meaningless if regarded as an 'asset' (Vermögen) but quite meaningful if regarded as an expression of 'debts'" (translated). Unfortunately, Cholerus did not tell us where Leonardo da Pisa made this remark. But if it was actually Leonardo's, it would confirm Scorgie's second argument against Peters and Emery [1978]. But it hardly meant a definite victory in the recognition of negative numbers in general. Most European mathematicians did not accept them as genuine numbers until the second half of the 19th century.[8] Eminent mathematicians, such as Nicholas Chuquet (1445?-1500?) and Michael Stifel (1486?-1567) called them "absurd;" Jerom Cardan (1501-1576) regarded negative roots (of equations) as mere symbols; François Vieta (also Viète, 1540-1603) abandoned negative numbers altogether; and Gottfried W. Leibniz (1646-1716) recognized them only from a *formal* point of view. On the other hand, Raphael Bombelli [1526-1572 or later] and Albert Girard (1595-1632), particularly in his *Invention novelle en algèbre* [1629], put negative and positive numbers on a par, as did Thomas Harriot (1560-1621). However, Harriot did *not* accept negative roots of equations in his posthumous work *Artis analyticae praxis* [1631]. John Wallis (1616-

[8]For details, see Kline [1980, pp. 114-116, 118-119, 153-155] and Boyer [1989, pp. 227, 245f, 256, 260, 312, 316, 321, 342f, 385, 416, 511].

1703) also accepted negative numbers as equal to positive ones. Yet, Jean d'Alembert (1717-1783) published an article in the famous *Encyclopédie*, edited by Denis Diderot and himself [1751-1759], under the title "Negative," which stated that "a problem leading to a negative solution means that some part of the hypothesis is false but assumed to be true" [quoted in Kline, 1980, p. 118]. Only Leonhard Euler (1707-1783) shared the Indians' position of vindicating negative numbers by reasserting that "we denote what a man really possesses by positive numbers, using, or understanding the sign +; whereas his debts are represented by negative numbers, or by using the sign - " [Euler, 1770, Ch. 2, item 17; p. 4 in the English reprint edition, 1972/1989].

At the end of the 18th century and the beginning of the 19th, mathematicians still continued to object to negative numbers. William Frend (1757-1841) [1796, preface] stated that a number "submits to be taken away from a number greater than itself but to attempt to take it away from a number less than itself is ridiculous;" Lazare Carnot (1753-1823) [1797/1970] affirmed that the idea of something being less than nothing is absurd; August De Morgan (1806-1871) [1831] likewise voiced his objections to negative numbers. William R. Hamilton (1805-1865) was hardly more favorably disposed toward negative numbers. Only toward the end of the 19th century was the mathematicians' conundrum with negative numbers, and rational and complex numbers in general, slowly resolved, as seen from the following quote from Kline [1980, p. 179]:

> The logic of the rational numbers was still missing. Dedekind realized this and, in *The Nature and Meaning of Numbers* [1888], he described the basic properties that one might use for an axiomatic approach to the rationals. Giuseppe Piano (1858-1932), utilizing Dedekind's ideas and some ideas in Hermann Grassmann's *Textbook on Arithmetic* [1861] succeeded in *Principles of Arithmetic* [1889] in producing a development of the rational numbers from axioms about the positive whole numbers. Thus, finally, the logical structure of the real and complex number systems was at hand.

By then, it was high time for mathematics to have caught up with humankind's perception of social and physical reality as, by the end of the 19th century, innumerable empirical applications for negative numbers had already been conceived (in fields from accounting and geography to thermodynamics and electricity).

THE HINDUS' ACCEPTANCE OF NEGATIVE NUMBERS AND THEIR INTERPRETATION AS DEBTS

The conservative European attitude toward negative numbers did not hold sway over Indian mathematicians who were not restrained by foundational considerations and proved to be more venturesome in operating with such magnitudes. Colebrooke's [1973] book and translation of two of Brahmagupta's chapters, "Gañitád'haya" and "Cuttacád'hyaya," are usually taken as evidence that Brahmagupta [628] was the first to have accepted negative numbers and operated with them.[9] Colebrooke's book also contains translations of two chapters, "Víjagañita" and "Lílávatí," by Bhāskara [1151] from which we can formulate our main hypothesis that Indian mathematicians, possibly due to a long-standing accounting tradition, seem to have been the first to give empirical meaning to *negative numbers* by interpreting them *as debts* (i.e., in terms of a basic accounting notion), while interpreting positive numbers as the *possession of assets*. The crucial evidence comes from two footnotes in Colebrooke's translation of Bhāskara's work. One of these, expressing the "rule for addition of affirmative and negative quantities," states: "For a demonstration of the rule, the [medieval] commentators, Súryadása and Crīshń, exhibit familiar examples of the comparison of debts and assets" [Colebrooke,1973, p. 131, note 2]. The other, the "rule for the subtraction of positive and negative quantities," said: "So in respect of chattels, that, to which a man bears the relation of owner [possession], is considered as positive in regard to him: and the converse (or negative quantity) is that to which another person has the relation of owner" [Colebrooke, 1973, p. 132, note 3].[10]

---

[9]See particularly item 17 and Statement of item 18 of Section I of Chapter XVIII on "Cuttacád' hyaya,"("Algebra") of Brahmagupta's book *Brahma-Sphuta-Sidd'hánta* [628], as well as items 31 and 32-33 of Section II of the same book and chapter.

[10] As to the modern usage of assigning minus signs in accounting, they are, of course, not only assigned to debt claims but also to ownership claims. But beware, the word "ownership" is often used in an ambiguous way, meaning either possession of an asset (the value of which would be expressed by a positive number) or the claim represented by an owner's equity (represented by a negative number).

It may also be noted that "debts" were not the Hindus' only interpretation

As to a better comprehension of the influence of Hindu accounting on the mathematical acceptance of negative numbers, the first section mentioned two prerequisites that might be formulated as auxiliary hypotheses. First, basic accounting notions, including asset, debt, revenues, expenses, and income, were first described in India in Kautilya's *Arthaśāstra* [ca. 300 B.C.], establishing a cultural climate that may ultimately have facilitated the association between a debt and a negative number. This claim can be verified from various presentations and translations of or commentaries on the *Arthaśāstra,* such as Shamasastry [1967], Kangle [1960, 1963, 1965], and Rangarajan [1992]. Relevant accounting interpretations and further commentaries can be found in Choudhury [1982], Bhattacharyya [1988], and Mattessich [1997, 1998b].

Kautilya's treatment of accounting was sophisticated enough to include (i) various types of income, including aspects of accounting for price and price-level changes and a possible distinction between what modern accountants call real vs. fictitious holding gains[11] and their potential relations to other accounting concepts; (ii) classifications of expenditures or costs, including possibly fixed and variable costs; and (iii) some notions of assets, debts, and capital. Thus, the description of accounting seems to have been more advanced in India than anywhere else at the time, with the possible exception of China. In consequence, the existence of cultural prerequisites for relating accounting to mathematics, particularly for attributing positive numbers to the possessions of assets but negative numbers to debts, seems to be more likely in such a sophisticated environment. This supposition is reinforced by a relative social stability and continuity in India from the 3rd century B.C. to early medieval times. Despite many terrible conflicts, it seems that during this time India did not experience anything comparable to the decline of the Roman Empire in the wake of devastating wars

---

of negative numbers. The note to Bhāskara's "Līlávatī" [par. 166], referring to a segment on a line or geographical direction, states: "The segment is negative, that is to say, is in the contrary direction. As the west is contrary of east; and the south the converse of north" [Colebrooke, 1973, p. 132, note 3].

[11]A fictitious holding gain merely appears to be a gain; it refers to holding a (non-monetary) commodity during an inflationary period in which, for example, the general price level increased equally or more than the specific price level pertaining to this commodity. Obviously, it is not possible to derive from mere inflation any real gain by holding a non-monetary asset (in contrast to owing a debt during such an inflationary time which, indeed, may result in a genuine holding gain).

and mass migrations. Thus, Indian insights into accounting during the 3rd century B.C., or even before, are likely to have been preserved until medieval times.

The second prerequisite or auxiliary hypothesis is that assets and debt claims are among the most basic accounting concepts. Debt claims, one of the earliest accounting notions, constitute the very pivot on which Sumerian token accounting of the 4th millennium B.C. hinged. This ancestry may be taken as further support that the accounting aspect of debt claims is at least as fundamental as its legalistic one. There exists incontrovertible archaeological evidence that the accounting notion of a debt — manifested by a kind of IOU in the form of a clay envelope (and, at times, more perishable receptacles) containing clay tokens that represented the items owed — preceded not only the codification of laws and legal regulation of debts, but even the invention of writing by at least 500 years. While archaeological findings of token accounting, i.e., clay tokens and envelopes representing debt and ownership claims, go back to the middle of the 4th millennium B.C., proto-cuneiform writing developed around 3000 B.C. [see, for example, Schmandt-Besserat, 1977, 1992; Mattessich, 1987, 1995, 1998b; Nissen et al., 1993; and Galassi, 1997]. The first known legal codes appeared about a millennium later; they are those of the kings of Isin and Shulgi (third dynasty of Ur, ca. 2000 B.C.) and King Lipit-Ishtar (2100 B.C. to 2092 B.C.) [see Ceram, 1949, p. 421], all of them precursors to the much better known code of Hammurabi, nowadays attributed to the 18th century B.C.

Even if the moral or quasi-legalistic aspect of a debt is a prerequisite to its accounting aspect, the former is so closely intertwined with the latter that in most social settings they occur conjointly.[12] What would a debt practically be without

---

[12]There is no evidence that five thousand years ago the Sumerians conceived of such distinct disciplines as law, accounting, and business administration. Thus, I wholly agree with one of the reviewers that historians should beware of attributing present circumstances to ancient times. But, it is quite a different matter when it comes to such basic human notions as having a "claim" on something or somebody, corresponding directly to our notions of assets and debts, liabilities and ownership. To deny that those relations existed among the Sumerians does not only run counter to the pertinent archaeological evidence, but also against the insights of anthropology and the behavioral sciences in general. Nietzsche [1887] traced even the origin of conscience to "the contractual relationship between *creditor* and *debtor*." Though this may be an interesting explanation, I suspect that the notion of conscience has older and deeper roots.

the two major ingredients of accounting — accountability
and counting? The *recording* of a debt becomes indispensable
for at least two reasons: (i) to provide for the limitations of
human memory and (ii) to substantiate the existence and
magnitude of the debt at due-date. This may explain why
some accounting tokens go back as far as 8000 B.C., five thousand years before the invention of writing. Yet, I have no
objection to one reviewer's suggestion that "the glory of
negative numbers should go to 'law' as much as 'accounting'." I might even go beyond and extend the "glory" to geography as well (cf., see the second paragraph of footnote 10).
However, in this venue, I deem it reasonable to concentrate
on accounting aspects. The major point of this paper is unaf-
fected; namely, that in medieval India the "existence" and
use of negative numbers were justified, though not exclusively, by interpreting them as "debts," which in turn were
conceived as "negative assets." Whether "debts" and "assets"
have further commercial and legal connotations is here beside the point.

Perhaps there is a third prerequisite to comprehending
the significance of accounting for this particular historical
impact on mathematics. Only those familiar with the enduring resistance of European mathematicians to negative numbers can fully appreciate the early Indian achievement of giving the concept of negative numbers its proper place in the
pantheon of mathematical concepts. Accounting seems to
have played its part in this achievement. Of course, had this
taken place in Europe, or had the Arabs and Leonardo da
Pisa succeeded in transferring this need for a mathematical
legitimization of negative numbers, Western mathematics
might well have advanced more rapidly.

Admittedly, the first part of my hypothesis is supported
by nothing but two short footnotes in a medieval mathematical or astronomical manuscript. Some readers might consider this fairly "slim" evidence. Accounting historians, in
contrast to archaeologists, dealing with later periods are
used to much more abundant evidential material and, thus,
might be prone to disparage the support for the hypothesis
here advanced. Yet comparing this with the diminutive
evidential basis on which major advances in modern
palaeontology frequently rests, one must admit that disre-
garding any kind of genuine evidence, be it as unobtrusive as

the one supporting my hypothesis, may deprive any science of worthwhile insights.[13] As to evaluation of this evidential support, it must ultimately lie with the reader. Measurement of such support is still elusive and subjectively tainted, particularly as far as hypotheses concerning early historical or prehistoric events are concerned. Here the decisive criterion for accepting a specific hypothesis is not the "absolute" strength of evidence, but how the support compares to the evidence propping the counter-hypothesis. The latter would consist, in our case, of the two-part view that, first, "debt" is *not* a basic accounting notion and, that second, the concept of "debt" did *not* have a part in facilitating or justifying the acceptance of negative numbers by major medieval Indian mathematicians.[14]

---

[13]Just as the DNA of a single human hair may constitute decisive forensic evidence in a criminal court, so a single medieval footnote or two may constitute evidence that "flips" the preference for a traditional hypothesis (e.g., the counter-hypothesis) to that for a new hypothesis. Thus, it is not so much the quantity but the quality of evidence that ultimately counts.

[14]I am reluctant to offer here any methodological recapitulation, but it seems necessary due to some misunderstanding raised during the review process of this paper. So far, neither Carnap [1950] nor anyone else has succeeded in establishing an *objective* measure of the "degree of confirmation" for measuring the strength with which a piece of specific evidence supports an hypothesis. Thus, it seems that one has to rely on Popper's [1935] assumption that a plausible hypothesis is accepted as long as no refutation is provided. As to "plausibility," it is rooted in a subjective "degree of belief" [cf., Ramsey, 1931] based on tangible evidence. The alternative of an "objective" measurement as, for example, the "degree of confirmation," first developed by Neyman and Pearson [1937] and widely used in statistical hypotheses testing, is restricted to statistical mass phenomena and, therefore, is not applicable to such historical hypotheses as advanced above. For further details see Mattessich [1978, Chs. 5 and 6, pp. 141-248].

Applying these insights to the present paper, one reaches the following twofold conclusion. First, the "link" between the evidence that relatively sophisticated accounting thoughts had existed in India since 300 B.C. and the hypothesis that it was the familiarity of medieval Indians with accounting which led them to interpret a debt as a negative asset, leading ultimately to the use of negative numbers in mathematics, cannot be established objectively but merely subjectively. Second, to invalidate this hypothesis, one has to show it impossible *that the relative accounting sophistication of early Hindu society* could have led to the pertinent influence upon medieval Indian mathematicians. Hence, this paper may well stimulate historians to continue their search for a genuine refutation of one or more of my hypotheses.

CONCLUSION

In mathematics it is not always the formal consistency alone that is decisive. In many situations the "Authority of Nature," as Kline [1980, p. 308] called it, is no less important. Although the empirical existence of a structure or relationship is not a prerequisite for its acceptance as a mathematical concept, it often happens that such existence stimulates the formulation of a concept. This seem to have happened in Sumeria and ancient Egypt when *special cases* of the "Pythagorean theorem" were formulated on the basis of experience, perhaps in large construction projects. Something similar may have happened when the Indians conceived the legitimacy of negative numbers on the basis of either debts as an inverse to the possession of assets or of opposite geographical directions (see footnote 10). Of course, one may also cite examples of reverse cases where mathematics was leading and empirical science following; e.g., the formulation of non-Euclidean geometry many decades before the discovery of the gravitational curvature of space by Einstein and Minkowski. But in the case of legitimizing negative numbers in Europe, the delay by many centuries showed its mathematicians limping much behind man's perception of reality.

The Arabs, and through them Leonardo da Pisa, might have transmitted to the West some knowledge about negative quantities; but the subsequent circumstances (greater "logical scruples" of European mathematicians and a more foundational-deductive orientation than the pragmatic one of their Indian counterparts [cf., Kline, 1980, pp. 110-112]), indicate that neither the Arabs nor Leonardo da Pisa succeeded in conveying the need for legitimizing negative numbers, though they did transmit such Indian achievements as the decimal place-order system and a symbol for zero.[15]

As demonstrated, it seems likely that the centuries-old accounting tradition of the medieval Hindus [see, e.g., Choudhury, 1982; Bhattacharyya, 1988; Mattessich, 1997, 1998a] facilitated this crucial achievement of accepting negative numbers. From an historical point of view, the fascinating details of the centuries-long struggle over the general acceptance of negative numbers and their first mathematical recognition

---

[15]The text by Aleksandrov et.al. [1963, p. 14] pointed out that in "a rudimentary form, zero already appears in the late Babylonian cuneiform writings, but its systematic introduction was an achievement of the Indians."

by the Indians seem hardly less significant than other relations between accounting and negative numbers (e.g., those that Peters and Emery asserted and Scorgie refuted).

Many centuries after the Indians had justified the use of negative numbers to represent debts, a quite similar justification can be found in the writings of the eminent mathematician Leonhard Euler [1770]. Regrettably, this interesting cultural contribution, of which our discipline has partaken through such a basic accounting notion as that of "debt," has hitherto received scant attention from accountants, even though mathematicians have occasionally reminded us. Aleksandrov et al. [1963, p. 39], for example, observed that the "Indians invented our present system of numeration. They also introduced negative numbers, comparing the contrast between positive and negative numbers with the contrast between property and debt or between two directions on a straight line." Likewise, Kline [1980, p. 110] concluded: "The Hindus have added to the logical woes of mathematicians by introducing negative numbers to represent debts. In such uses positive numbers represent assets."

REFERENCES

Aleksandrov, A. D., Kolmogorov, A. N., and Lavrent'ev, M. A. (1963), *Mathematics — Its Content, Methods and Meaning*, Vol. 1, Gould, S. H. and Bartha, T. (trans.) (Cambridge, MA: M.I.T. Press), original Russian version (Moscow: 1956).

Bhāskara (1151), *Áchárya* (India).

Bhattacharyya, Anjan K. (1988), *Modern Accounting Concepts in Kautilya's Arthaśāstra* (Calcutta: Firma KLM Private Ltd.).

Brahmagupta (628), *Brahma-Sphuta-Sidd'hánta* (India).

Boyer, Carl B. (1989), *A History of Mathematics* (New York: John Wiley & Sons, 1989).

Cajori, Florian (1919), *A History of Mathematics*, revised edition (New York: Macmillan).

Carnap, Rudolf (1950), *Logical Foundations of Probability* (Chicago: University of Chicago Press).

Carnot, Lazare N. M. (1970), *Réflexions sur la métaphysique du calcul infinitésimal* (Paris: Albert Blanchard), reprint of 1797 edition.

Ceram, C. W. (1949), *Götter, Gräber und Gelehrte* (Hamburg: Rowolt Verlag — Lizenzausgabe Bertelsmann Lesering).

Cholerus, E. (1944), *Von Pythagoras bis Hilbert* (Vienna: Karl H. Bischoff Verlag).

Choudhury, N (1982), "Aspects of Accounting and Internal Control — India 4th Century B.C.," *Accounting and Business Research*, Vol. 12, No. 46: 105-110.

Colebrooke, Henry T. (1973), *Algebra with Arithmetic and Mensuration from Sanskrit of Brahmegupta and Bháscara* (Wiesbaden: Martin Sändig), original edition (London: John Murray, 1817).

Cooper, William W. and Ijiri, Yuji (eds.) (1983), *Kohler's Dictionary for Accountants* (Englewood Cliffs, NJ: Prentice-Hall, Inc.).

d'Alembert, Jean Le Rond (1751-1759), "Negative," in Diderot, D. and d'Alembert, J. (eds.), *Encyclopédie* (Paris).

Dedekind, J. W. Richard (1888), *Was sind und was sollen die Zahlen?* (Braunschweig), translated in Beman, Woodruff Wooster (ed.), *Essays on the Theory of Numbers* (Chicago: 1901).

De Morgan, August (1831), *On the Study and Difficulties of Mathematics* (London: Library of Useful Knowledge).

Diderot, Denis and d'Alembert, Jean Le Rond (eds.) (1751-1759), *Encyclopédie* (Paris).

Euler, Leonhard (1770), *Anleitung zur Algebra* (Germany), English reprint edition: Hewlett, J. (trans.), *Elements of Algebra* (New York: Springer-Verlag, 1972/1989).

Frend, William (1796), *Principles of Algebra* (London).

Galassi, Giuseppe (1997), "Recenti sviluppi dell' archeologia della Ragioneria — I contibuti di Denise Schmandt-Besserat e di Richard Mattessich," *Storia della Ragioneria*, Vol. 0 (Roma: Società Italiana della Storia Ragioneria).

Girard, Albert (1629), *Invention novelle en algèbre* (Paris).

Grassmann, Hermann (1861), *Textbook on Arithmetic* (Germany).

Grassmann, Hermann (1889), *Principles of Arithmetic* (Germany).

Harriot, Thomas (1631), *Artis analyticae praxis* (Paris).

Kangle, R. P. (1960), *The Kautilya Arthaśāstra, Part I, A Critical (Sanskrit) Edition with a Glossary* (Bombay: University of Bombay), later edition, 1969.

Kangle, R. P. (1963), *The Kautilya Arthaśāstra, Part II, An English Translation with Critical and Explanatory Notes* (Bombay: University of Bombay), later edition, 1972.

Kangle, R. P. (1965), *The Kautilya Arthaśāstra, Part III, A Study [in English]* (Bombay: University of Bombay).

Kautilya, Vishnugupta (ca. 300 B.C.), *Arthaśāstra* (India/Magadha).

Kline, Morris (1980), *Mathematics — the Loss of Certainty* (Oxford: Oxford University Press).

Leonardo da Pisa (1202), *Liber Abaci* (Pisa).

Mattessich, Richard (1978), *Instrumental Reasoning and Systems Methodology: An Epistemology of the Applied and Social Sciences* (Dordrecht/Boston, MA: D. Reidel Publishing Co.).

Mattessich, Richard (1987), "Prehistoric Accounting and the Problem of Representation: On Recent Archeological Evidence of the Middle East from 8000 B.C. to 3000 B.C.," *Accounting Historians Journal*, Vol. 14, No. 2: 71-91, reprinted in Lee, T. A. (ed.) (1990), *The Closure of the Accounting Profession*, Vol. 1 (New York: Garland Press): 246-266.

Mattessich, Richard (1995), *Critique of Accounting — Examination of the Foundations and Normative Structure of an Applied Discipline* (Westport, CT: Quorum Books, Greenwood Publishing Group).

Mattessich, Richard (1997), "Aspects of Early Accounting Systems (after 3000 B.C.)," abstract, in Richardson, Alan J. (ed.), *Disorder and Harmony: 20th Century Perspectives on Accounting History* (Vancouver, B.C.: CGA Canada Research Foundation): 337-338.

Mattessich, Richard (1998a), "Review and Extension of Bhattacharyya's *Modern Accounting Concepts in Kautilya's Arthasāstra*," *Accounting, Business and Financial History*, Vol. 8, No. 2: 191-209.

Mattessich, Richard (1998b), "Recent Insights into Mesopotamian Accounting of the 3rd Millennium B.C. — Successor to Token Accounting," *Accounting Historians Journal*, Vol. 25, No. 1: 1-27.

Neyman, J. and Pearson, E. S. (1937), "On the Problem of the Most Efficient Tests of Statistical Hypotheses," *Philosophical Transactions of the Royal Society*, Series A 236: 263-294.

Nietzsche, Friederich (1887), *Genealogie der Moral* (Germany).

Nissen, H. J., Damerow, Peter, and Englund, R. K. (1993), *Archaic Bookkeeping — Early Writing Techniques of Economic Administration in the Ancient Near East* (Chicago: University of Chicago Press).

Pacioli, Luca (1494), *Summa de arithmetica, geometria, proportioni et proportionalita* (Venice).

Peters, Richard M. and Emery, Douglas R. (1978), "The Role of Negative Numbers in the Development of Double Entry Bookkeeping," *Journal of Accounting Research*, Vol. 16, No. 2: 424-426.

Popper, Karl (1935), *Logic der Forschung* (Tübingen: J.C.B. Mohr), translated as *The Logic of Discovery* (New York: Basic Books, 1959).

Ramsey, Frank P. (1931), "Truth and Probability," in Braithwaite, Richard B. (ed.), *Foundations of Mathematics and Other Logical Essays* (London: Kegan Paul).

Rangarajan, L. N. (ed.) (1992), *Kautilya—The Arthasāstra* (New Delhi: Penguin Books).

Schmandt-Besserat, Denise (1977), "An Archaic Recording System and the Origin of Writing," *Syro-Mesopotamian Studies*, Vol. 1, No. 2: 1-32.

Schmandt-Besserat, Denise (1992), *Before Writing. Vol. I: From Counting to Cuneiform; Vol. II: A Catalogue of Near Eastern Tokens* (Austin, TX: University of Texas Press).

Scorgie, Michael E. (1989), "'The Role of Negative Numbers in the Development of Double Entry Bookkeeping': A Comment," *Journal of Accounting Research*, Vol. 27, No. 2: 316-318.

Shamasastry, R. (1967), *Kautilya's Arthasāstra*, 8th edition (Mysore: Mysore Printing and Publishing House), reprint of 1915 edition.

Sun-Tsu (1st century) *Sun-Tsu Suan-ching* (China).

Vogel, Kurt (1970), "Fibonacci" in Gillispie, Charles C. (ed.) (1970-1990), *Dictionary of Scientific Biography*, Vol. 4 (New York: Scribner): 604- 613.

Youschkevitch, A. P. (1970), "Abul-Wafa . . ." in Gillispie, Charles C. (ed.) (1970-1990), *Dictionary of Scientific Biography*, Vol. 1 (New York: Scribner): 39-43.

List of Errata

p. 33/ Note 12/ line 2:"Hintika" should be "Hintikka".

p. 41/ Reference entry for: "Jasmin, S.A." should be "Jasim, S.A.".

p. 150/ Note 14/ Line 4 from bottom: "Ritchl" should be "Ritschl".

p. 152/ insert: Metha, Usha and Usha Takkar (1980), *Kautilya and His Arthaśāstra, New Delhi:* S. Chand.

p. 158/ Footnote 1/ line 4: "Abu'l Wefa" should be "Abu' Wafa".

p. 163/ line 5/ of quotation: "Piano" should be "Peano".

Index